The Steps We Took

The Steps We Took

A teacher of the Twelve Steps shares his experience, strength, and hope with all those recovering from addictions, all who want to recover, and all who love them.

by Joe McQ.

of "The Big Book Study Tapes"

August House Publishers, Inc.

ATLANTA

Published 1990 by August House, Inc.
augusthouse.com

Printed in the United States of America

31 30 29 PB

LIBRARY OF CONGRESS CATALOGING-IN-PUBLICATION DATA
McQ., Joe, 1928 - 2007
The steps we took : a teacher of the twelve steps shares his experience, strength, and hope with all people recovering from addictions, all who want to recover, and all who love them / by Joe McQ.
p. cm.
Includes bibliographical references (p.182)
ISBN 978-0-87483-151-1
1. Alcoholics—Religious life. 2. Narcotic addicts—Religious life.
3. Compulsive behavior—Patients—Religious life.
4. Twelve-step programs. I. Title.
BV4596.A48M36 1990
362.29'286—dc20 90-641

Executive editor: Ted Parkhurst
Project editor: Judith Faust
Cover Design: Wendell E. Hall
Production artwork: Ira Hocut
Design Direction: Ted Parkhurst

AUGUST HOUSE, INC. PUBLISHERS ATLANTA

To the first one hundred
and all who followed

And ye shall know the truth,
and the truth shall make you free.

John 8:32

Acknowledgments

The author and the editors are grateful to the following for their contributions to this book:

...Alcoholics Anonymous World Services, Inc., for permission to use the Steps;

...The board of the Kelly Foundation for their support of the project and for permission to use illustrations and adapt some text from *Recovery Dynamics;*

...Pat Caffey, Nancy Hampton, Martha Binz, Gayle Bostick, Velda Keeney, Darryl Haley, Kevin Clark, and Keith Lundy;

...Charlie P., Don A., Angie B., Bob B., and Kathy J.;

...All the folks at August House, particularly Judith Faust, Ted Parkhurst, and Liz Parkhurst;

...Most of all, to the two people who had the most to put up with while we were absorbed in the work and who loved and supported us anyway—Molly C. and Loubelle McQ.

Joe McQ., Sally C., & Huey C.

Contents

A Note from the Editors

I asked Joe about a year ago, "Do you remember when you were new in the program and getting insights?" He looked at me quizzically and said, "Oh, I'm still getting insights."

Although Joe has been a student of the Steps for close to 28 years, he would be quick to emphasize that he is still growing in their principles. But during these 28 years, Joe has become more and more a teacher of the Steps.

Working with individuals and with groups, he has shared his "experience, strength, and hope" with thousands and thousands of people through telling his story, through Step talks, through Big Book study and Big Book study tapes, through the treatment facility he has run for 20 years. In his text and materials for counselor/client use in treatment settings, he has taught others how to teach the program. Though he would not say it of himself, Joe has become a master teacher of these principles. Most important, like all good teachers, he practices the principles he teaches.

Joe has a wealth of insight and experience to share; he has been willing to share both. He is tireless in doing so, traveling almost every weekend to places near and far, all over the world. Many people have heard him in person or on tape. We hope this book will help more people "hear" him.

Whether or not you have heard Joe, we do hope you will "hear" him in these pages. The book came about by our taping a series of talks with Joe in our home. He came over, week after week, visited with our daughter (and her cats, one of whom he dubbed the "serenity cat"), sat in a rocking chair with a cup of decaf at his side, and talked. We listened, talked back, and asked questions. We all three laughed a good bit and generally enjoyed ourselves.

In going from the tapes to what you see on the page, we have tried to keep Joe's voice and his presence. We have done some rearranging and revising and a little adding, but most of what is here is straight from Joe.

We have been blessed in having this opportunity to work with Joe, and it is in that spirit—the spirit of blessing—that we offer this work to you. We pray that God may go before this book, be in it, and use it to bring you to greater freedom and wholeness.

Sally C. & Huey C.
Little Rock, Arkansas
February 1990

Introduction

Many people consider the Twelve Steps one of the greatest miracles of the twentieth century. You know, the Big Book, *Alcoholics Anonymous,* is now written in eighteen different languages. There's no telling how many lives have been touched by *Alcoholics Anonymous* and the essence of Alcoholics Anonymous—the Twelve Steps.

When God created the world and everything in it, He created it with a set of principles that wouldn't change, principles that govern everything including human life. During the course of history, our Creator has many times reminded us of these principles. They have been handed down through every great religion—Christianity, Islam, Buddhism, Judaism, Hinduism. All of them, even the lesser known religions of the peoples that we consider more "primitive," have had these principles revealed to them.

In 1935, with the creation of Alcoholics Anonymous, these principles were given to people again. This time they were given to a group of alcoholics with the aid of some people (The Oxford Groups) who were trying to revive first century Christianity. These recovering alcoholics, with divine guidance, boiled down the principles of living into twelve simple Steps. The Steps were clear and uncluttered with any theology. They worked for forty people through a word-of-mouth program. Once these simple Steps were written down, they spread around the world, and through them millions of people have been able to recover from alcoholism.

Then people with other addictions began to use them in their lives. I have read that there are 160 different groups in which people are helping each other by working these Steps. There are certainly more people being helped by the Steps than by more conventional, professional therapy. In fact, any problem we see in our lives can be healed with the Steps. The problems we see are usually symptoms, and the Twelve Steps address the underlying causes of our problems.

The exciting thing about the Twelve Steps is that they teach us how to live. Once we know the design of living and the principles of living a successful life, we find that we not only get over the problems we see, but we avoid many other problems we would have had. To me, the miracle is that all this was boiled down into twelve simple Steps which anybody can apply.

My idea in this book is to talk about these Steps, about how they are the principles of living, the steadfast and never-changing universal laws undoubtedly established by something beyond man. These principles that apply to human behavior are as dependable as the principles that govern physics. Sometimes we might imagine that *just once* water wouldn't freeze at 32 degrees, but no matter where we are, it always does. When God made water He made a governing principle, and that principle is dependable because it is unchanging. The same is true of the principles that govern human behavior. If we understand the principles which God has made to govern our lives, we can accomplish more and live better lives. Yet most of us know more about the principles that govern nature than we do about the principles that govern our own lives!

There are few people in our society who seem able or willing to teach us the principles. I think the family and the church and all the institutions that could be teaching the principles stopped many years ago, and started making rules. It's easier to give rules than it is to teach principles. But when you don't know the principles, you usually can't help but break the rules, sometimes all the rules. If you have the principles, you don't really need rules. That's what is great about the Twelve Steps. They aren't rules. The Twelve Steps don't have "don'ts"; they have "dos." That's what principles are: guidelines for what to do. The Twelve Steps are principles to live by.

It comes down basically to surrender. The Twelve Steps teach us that successful living is being in harmony with God and our fellow man. It is putting ourselves to maximum service of God and our fellow man. The reward is simple: it's harmony... it's happiness...it's contentment.

Joe McQ.
Little Rock, Arkansas
February 1990

The Twelve Steps

Here are the steps we took, which are suggested as a program of recovery.

1. We admitted we were powerless over alcohol—that our lives had become unmanageable.
2. Came to believe that a Power greater than ourselves could restore us to sanity.
3. Made a decision to turn our will and our lives over to the care of God *as we understood Him.*
4. Made a searching and fearless moral inventory of ourselves.
5. Admitted to God, to ourselves, and to another human being the exact nature of our wrongs.
6. Were entirely ready to have God remove all these defects of character.
7. Humbly asked Him to remove our shortcomings.
8. Made a list of all the people we had harmed, and became willing to make amends to them all.
9. Made direct amends to such people wherever possible, except when to do so would injure them or others.
10. Continued to take personal inventory and when we were wrong promptly admitted it.
11. Sought through prayer and meditation to improve our conscious contact with God *as we understood Him,* praying only for knowledge of His will for us and the power to carry that out.
12. Having had a spiritual awakening as the result of these Steps, we tried to carry this message to alcoholics, and to practice these principles in all our affairs.

Alcoholics Anonymous, 3d edition,
New York: Alcoholics Anonymous
World Services, Inc., 1976, pp. 59-60.

Neither the author nor the editors of *The Steps We Took* are speaking for Alcoholics Anonymous, or for any group thereof, or for any other Twelve-Step group.

What is the Problem?

We can become so caught up in a problem that all we can see to do is to try harder—try to get the wrong method to bring the right results by doing it harder!...Step 1 tells us we'd better stop and name the problem, and become willing to admit defeat before we rush in to fix things.

Step 1: We admitted we were powerless over..., that our lives had become unmanageable.

The truth is that many of the problems we have in life we can't fix. We are powerless over a whole lot of things. Step 1 is about being powerless, about not being able to fix everything. It's simple: sometimes we have to say, "I can't fix it."

Throughout our lives, we find ourselves powerless in certain situations. For example, we are powerless over other people. A lot of us are like the guy who doesn't realize that he is powerless over his co-workers. He goes to work day after day, year after year, trying to change them. This foolishness may go on for twenty-five years, or he may lose his job because of it—but he goes there eight hours a day trying to straighten those people out. If he would admit that he is powerless, the situation might get better. If he admitted his powerlessness over other people, his situation might get better on its own.

It was insanity for me that I tried for sixteen years in every way I could to drink normally. All I had to do was admit that I couldn't do it. What is this insanity, what is this drive within us that makes us want to try to do what we cannot—whether it's drinking or using or controlling others?

One thing that makes us "insane" is *self*—especially self-will and self-reliance. It doesn't seem to matter what race or even what gender we are, we humans are often the victims of "macho" thinking, that is, self-reliance. I think Jesus may have been teaching the principle of the first Step when He said, "Deny thyself." He meant, "Give up on yourself as the answer. Give up on self-reliance."

Let me use an example. My wife used to save her Green Stamps until she could get the premiums from the Green Stamp store. It never failed—everything she brought home had to be put together. Now, these things always came with clear instructions (principles) telling you step-by-step how to put whatever it was together. They would be ABC instructions, so simple they would insult a person of my intelligence. And it never failed that I would throw them in the garbage can and proceed to do it my way. After a while, I would be mad and frustrated trying to do it on my own and without the instructions. As soon as I'd see my wife looking the other way, I'd dig the instructions out of the egg shells and coffee grounds and lower myself to follow the principles until I got the thing put together.

When I'm trying to put something together, I may be trying to drive a tapered peg into a hole wrong end first. I keep hammering and hammering, but the thing won't go. I drive and force and maybe I'll finally look at the peg and say, "This peg won't go that way." Then I'll turn it around. But I can't turn it around until I admit that I've been trying to do it the wrong way.

Of course, as long as I persist in taking wrong actions, I'm going to get wrong results. (Or as Ernie Larsen puts it, "If nothing changes, nothing changes.") I have to admit that I was doing it wrong and turn the peg around before I can accomplish what I want to. As long as your mind tells you that's the way it goes, you can't do anything else. Somebody can be standing beside you saying, "Hey, turn that around!" but you can't do differently. We can get so caught up in a problem that all we can see to do is to *try harder—try to get the wrong method to bring the right results by doing it harder!*

And we do this, we persist, because we want to be in control and self-reliant. We don't want to admit defeat.

We humans are not meant to depend on our individual selves; we are meant to rely on each other. God didn't intend for us to be self-reliant; we are designed, as our principles spell out, to rely on each other. And we are designed to rely on God. We want to be self-propelled, but we can't be. Human beings surely aren't capable of operating without energy from God and from each other. In Step 1, we give up on being self-propelled, self-directed, and self-reliant.

Another part of our "insanity" is our blindness to reality. The story is told of a guy who had two horses. It worried him that he couldn't tell them apart. So finally he cropped one's tail, and he said that worked for a while but the tail grew back. Then he thought he would mark one horse's hooves with chalk, and that worked for a while—until the horse walked through some water. Finally, his son got a letter from him saying, "Well, son, I've finally figured out how to tell those two horses apart: I've discovered that the white one is four inches taller than the black one." Sometimes we are so blinded by a problem that we can't even begin to see the truth. We can't imagine any alternative to the ways we've been unsuccessfully trying to solve our problem.

Once we give up on a problem—any problem—and realize we are powerless over it, then we can make changes in ourselves. But we can't make any changes in ourselves until we see that we are powerless. This is really the key. Until we realize we are powerless over the situation, whatever it is, we can't begin to believe, we can't see the need to make new decisions or to make changes. We can't see any *possibility* of making new decisions or changes in our lives.

Admitting our powerlessness is how we accept that we do have a problem and begin to discover what the problem is. In some cases we are going to find out that there is a better action to take, that we have been doing it the wrong way. In some cases we may discover there is nothing we can do—we are powerless over the situation. (Sometimes this is really hard; if our child or our spouse is having a problem, it is very hard to admit or accept that we can't fix it.) In either case—whether we take a better action or admit that there is nothing we can do—we are on the road to recovery.

The process of Step 1, then, is twofold: to name the problem and to admit defeat. Even when we are just willing to say, "It doesn't fit that way, but I can turn it around," even that simple statement is admitting defeat.

If we humans could just realize that we are only on this earth a very short period of time. In the expanse of time, we are just an insignificant little dot. We pick up an insignificant amount of information and get a little bit of education, but there is no way that in such a short period of time we are going to pick up enough information to run our lives. It wasn't in God's plan. He didn't create us that way. He didn't give us the equipment for that. If you could take all the knowledge in all the minds in all the earth and put it in one brain, you still wouldn't have a significant percentage of the knowledge possible in the world. That super brain still would hardly know anything. It would be an enormous relief if we would realize this.

This is not to say we should not educate ourselves or learn as much as we can, but we have to realize that we will never *be* everything or *know* everything. When we realize our powerlessness, we can seek a source of Power.

Sometimes the answer to our problem lies in the little bit of knowledge we *do* have, so we go ahead and use it. But often we run into problems completely baffling to us, and then we must admit our powerlessness and turn to a Higher Power for assistance.

We need to get this straight: we have the Power. We have access to the Power to solve any problem—I mean *any* problem—in our lives.

If we go back to the Serenity Prayer...

> God, grant me the serenity
> to accept the things I cannot change
> courage to change the things I can
> and wisdom to know the difference...

we can put every problem on one side or the other: a situation can either be accepted or it can be changed. If we are powerless over it, we have to first accept it—*then* we can do something about it. But if we have a situation that we *need to change* and we are *trying to accept it,* we are just making it worse.

The greatest truth in the Serenity Prayer is "Grant me...wisdom to know the difference," to know which side to put it on. We need to realize that *on our own, we don't even have that.* We don't even know whether to accept things or change things, so we ask Him for the wisdom to know which is which. I've spent a lot of my life trying to change things I should have been accepting, and trying to accept things I could have changed—but was too stubborn to ask for help with!

Some way or other, all of us who are in the recovery process were given the wisdom to take that very first Step 1; that's what separates us from those who are still out there suffering. We surely weren't capable of doing it ourselves. We accepted the fact that we couldn't change without help, and we asked for the help. Likewise, some of us try for years to change a behavior, to try to become "normal" in some area, but we can't change. We give up, and accept the fact that we are not normal in this regard, and the behavior changes immediately.

We need to recall that God's will never enters where self-will dominates. As long as we insist on having our own will, there is no knowledge or concept of God's will. That's all the admission of powerlessness is. It is a shutting-off of self-will in a particular area.

Surrender usually means admitting we are powerless over "this thing." Of course, it is very hard for us to do this. Alcoholics, for example, must say, "I'm powerless over alcohol." Al-Anons and ACOAs (adult children of alcoholics) say, "I am powerless over people, places, and things." And you know all of us could say, "I'm powerless over that obnoxious person at work" or "over the carburetor on my car." We have to surrender all these things to God, and we have to *let go of outcomes.*

A lot of people see surrender as a weakness, but those of us who have had some experience with surrender know that it is the way we get true strength. All the people who are remembered as successful military commanders, for example, had one thing in common: they knew how to surrender or retreat. Custer didn't, MacArthur did.

We've got to learn the value of saying "I don't know" or "I made a mistake" or "what I've been trying doesn't work." People talk about surrender as if it were a very painful experience, and I guess it is painful at first, but we don't want to throw that tool away after we have used it on alcohol or another addiction. It is a powerful and useful tool we can use every day in our lives. For example, you know that if you're trying to reason with another human being who doesn't want to hear your reasoning, you are in an impossible situation. If you can surrender and admit you are powerless, probably in the long run something is going to bring that person to see the truth.

Although conventional wisdom says that to admit defeat is some kind of failure, it certainly isn't. In fact, it opens the door to success. What we are talking about here, with these principles called the Twelve Steps, is *unconventional wisdom.*

For example, to illustrate the necessity of giving up, I often ask people the question, "What is the first thing you have to do if you want to get a new car?" Usually they'll say something like "go to the bank" or "go pick one out." I say, "No, it isn't. The first thing you have to do is give up on the old one."

Step 1 opens the door to Step 2. I like to use the parable of the prodigal son (Luke 15:11-32) to illustrate this Step. The prodigal son let self-will run the show. He had an inheritance coming so he said, "Give me mine." And he went out and spent his money on wine, women, and song, and then he got into trouble. He was down there eating the husks off the corn with the hogs, but he was telling himself, "This ain't so bad. My ship will probably come in next week or things will get better somehow." But somehow he was given a moment of truth, no doubt from a Power greater than himself, and he became able to see reality. He said to himself, "Look, I'm in the hog pen." There was probably some other guy standing nearby who said, "Hell, man, you've been down there six months." But he didn't know he was down there until he had a moment of reality. As soon as he did he said, "The servants at my father's house are eating better than I am." As soon as he had this moment of reality, as soon as he was able to see the truth, he was able to make a decision to give up his self-will. He went back to his father and everything was restored to him. But he could easily have stayed there and died without that moment of truth, of insight.

One of the things we can't see when we are blocked off from reality is that whatever our problem is, millions of people before us have solved the same problem! The first Step is really much like the first verse of the Beatitudes: "Blessed are the poor in spirit"...those who can admit they are powerless and need the help of God and other people..."for theirs is the kingdom of heaven." (Matthew 5:3)

If we want something fixed "this way," we are only going to see it "this way." We won't see the other possibilities. When the opportunity to fix the thing another way comes open, we won't recognize it. In other words, when we tell God how we want something fixed, we really haven't given up or turned the problem over at all.

Often the solutions to problems are beyond our imagination. Everything in my life—my work, who I am, everything—has been built on what I thought was the worst thing in my life: my alcoholism. When I surrendered to that, my life changed in ways that I could never have imagined.

This Step, the first Step, has to be taken one hundred percent. All the others can be done imperfectly at first and the program will still work, but the first Step has to be taken one hundred percent. It's like damming up water: if you dam it up ninety-nine percent, the dam will break. But if the water is dammed up one hundred percent, it will be forced to seek another way out.

The first Step is about surrender, the surrender involved in facing the truth. Father John Doe says that Step 1 is the only non-spiritual Step. We have to make it alone. But I believe the ability to make it is a grace because there are too many people who die without ever making it. It's about finally facing the truth of a situation. The Bible says, "...ye shall know the truth, and the truth shall make you free." (John 8:32) In Step 1 we are just about to begin getting free.

There is a Solution Beyond Ourselves

This is what sanity is: the ability to see the truth. And if we can see the truth, then we will be free from the problem.

Step 2: Came to believe that a Power greater than ourselves could restore us to sanity.

Once we see that we can't handle a problem ourselves, a whole new set of possibilities opens up. Then we can look at avenues beyond ourselves. We don't have access to those possibilities as long as we are trying to solve everything *within* ourselves.

So the second principle is the solution, which we can come to after we surrender. As we have said, surrendering means saying that something is beyond our control. Surrendering puts us in a position for a different alternative.

Step 2 means we can now look for a solution. Sometimes our solution is beyond ourselves. Let's use the example of a car again: something may go wrong with the car and we may try to figure out what is wrong with it. We may say, "Oh, it's just the gas," or "It's just the road." But we can't do anything about it—and this kind of behavior is sometimes just a form of denial—until we either fix it or admit that it is beyond our ability to fix and turn it over to someone who can fix it. We have to first believe that there is an answer and then believe that we can have access to the answer.

Believing is the state of mind we must have before we can begin any project. It is an individual force that we all have. Believing defines the limits of our lives. We can't get any more education than we believe we can; we can't make any more money than we believe we can.

Belief is an awesome force. Everybody has it, but what matters is how we use it and apply it in our lives. A few years ago, I went out to the Black Hills in South Dakota to Mount Rushmore. I looked at that incredible carving of those four presidents in that gigantic mountain, and I wondered how the sculptor, Gutzon Borglum, ever came to believe he could do a difficult thing like that. It's the same with the Wright Brothers and Christopher Columbus as with Gutzon Borglum.

I always say that believing is an eternal force, a lighthouse that stays on all the time. There is no way to turn it off; so if we don't use it *for* ourselves, then we have to use it *against* ourselves. For example, there are people down on their luck who have had to apply to the state for a little assistance. But instead of recovering, they sit there feeling sorry for themselves and come to believe that the little amount of money the state gives them each month is all they are worth. They sit there and gripe and complain, and they develop this state of mind, this belief. The result, of course, is that their self-esteem is eroded.

Believing is a choice. Believing is a tentative place. It's a place to begin, even without convictions. I think the greatest difficulty we have with believing is that we want something with more certainty to start with; we want more assurance. We expect faith before we start, but believing comes first. It is not faith at the beginning; it's speculation or suspicion, and that's really all you can expect right then, because believing is the beginning point.

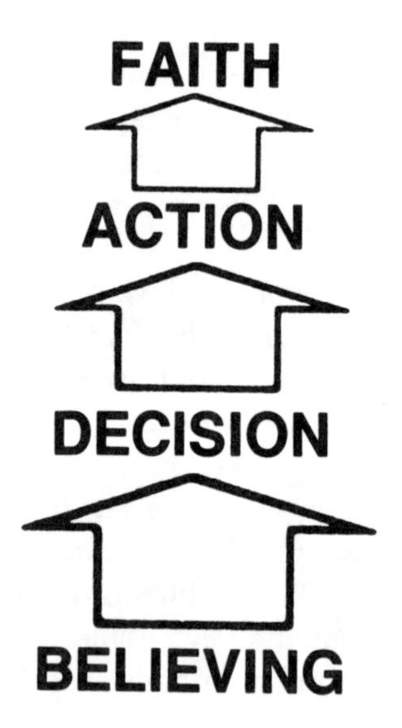

It was the beginning for the Wright Brothers; it was the

beginning for Christopher Columbus. It was the beginning for the Empire State Building and for Mount Rushmore. Everything man has accomplished began in his mind; he had to first believe that he could do something. We usually think the beginning of a project happens on the day the foundation is laid, but actually it began long before that, in someone's mind, when he or she came to believe that the thing was possible.

We use this every day, and we see the results of it. We don't see the power of believing; we can only see the results of believing. But we see these results everywhere we look!

Each and every one of us has this power of believing, and no two people have it alike. (See Appendix 2, Religious Beliefs.) I think that it is surely guided or directed by some force beyond ourselves. Because if each of us believed the same, each of us would accomplish the same things. So it is given to us on an individual basis to produce an individual talent to provide a certain service in this world. It's not so much our ability; it's a spirit; it's guidance.

God plants within us the seeds of the tasks that He wants done. Each person can believe that he can accomplish his specific role in the plan for the world. That's our job. The happiest a person is ever going to be in life is when he is accomplishing those tasks. But a person who is dependent on a substance such as alcohol or drugs, or who is dependent on someone else, doesn't have the freedom to use that power of believing.

Sometimes, though, we are affected—inhibited—by what other people think. Everybody thought Columbus was crazy because they *knew* the world was flat. So they said, "You can't do that. You can see the world is flat; just look." But he dared to believe differently.

When we are searching for a way out, we are like a mouse in a maze. You can put a mouse in a maze, and when he comes up against a wall, he will search for alternatives until he finally works his way through the maze and gets out. If you ever put him in there again, he will remember the right way and go right through. He believes one route will get him where he wants to go, and he finds out that choice was wrong, so he tries some alternate way. That's how we do it, too. Our believing might be wrong, but if we believe wrong and decide wrong and run into bad situations, *all we have to do is come back and change what we believe and try again until we are finally successful.* One advantage the mouse has, though, is that once he makes a mistake, he won't make it again. A human being is so emotional that he will make the same mistake over and over and maybe never find the right way out. (And we're supposed to be superior because of our "rational" minds!)

Believing is an important spiritual principle, a spiritual tool. Everybody has the power to use it—everybody. But believing and not acting on your belief is not much good. If you believe in God and still run your own life, it isn't going to do you any good. If people tell me they have believed in God all their lives and they are still in a mess, I say, "The devils probably believe in God, too." Lots of people believe in God because they think it's what nice people do, but if you don't *use* it, then your belief is not effective.

Believing is the state of the mind preceding all action, good or bad. This Step says, "Came to believe that a Power greater than ourselves...." We have to come to believe that there is an answer. Then we can give the mind a command. When your mind is given a command by the power of believing, you direct the energy and begin to search—and you will find the solution. The human mind is an awesome thing. First we have to believe there is an answer to our problem, or believe we can see the truth (because that is what sanity is: the ability to see the truth). And if we can see the truth, then we will be free from the problem.

Jesus said, "...ye shall know the truth, and the truth shall make you free." (John 8:32) Truth sets us free from the lie which is insanity. Each of us is constantly seeing the truth. None of us sees the truth *whole;* only God can do that. We have an interpretation of the truth which we can see, and yet many times our interpretation of the truth runs us right back into the lie (the insanity). *The truth has got to come from somewhere beyond us.* The power of believing is plugging in to begin to find that truth. Everybody, if you ask, will tell you they are proceeding from the truth, and they are—from the truth as they see it. A person has to examine, really examine, his perception of the truth, and do it frequently.

I think from the very first Step—surrender—we start to get it. Because surrender produces the power of believing. There is no way you can see or believe the truth until you have surrendered your old perception of the truth. *Change actually begins with surrender, because you can't see another alternative until you surrender your way of doing things.* Then the dominoes start to fall.

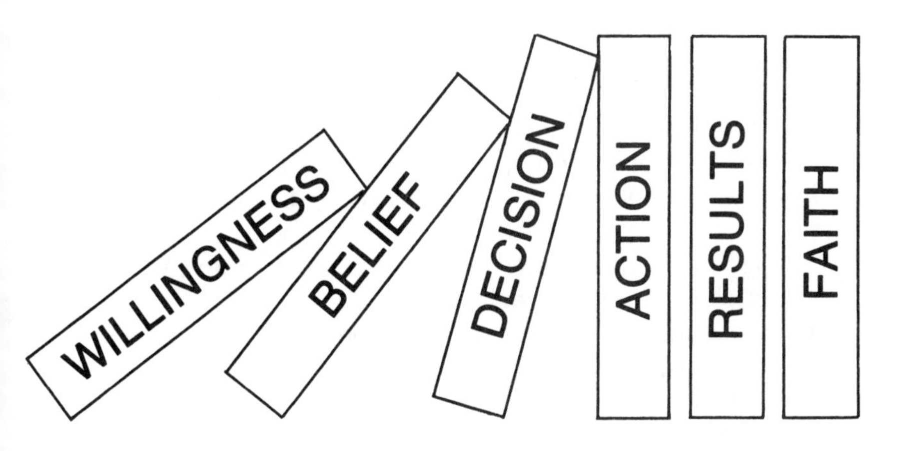

It's as if you set up a row of dominoes. You push over the first one, and it knocks over the second one, and it knocks down the third one, and so on and on. But there is really no more energy needed after the first domino. All the energy comes from the first Step. And every time we take the first Step again, we generate all that energy all over again.

Surrender is understood as such a negative word. Most people think it means that you have lost the whole war. But a good general knows how to surrender when it's to his own advantage and he can come out in a better position. When we see that we are defeated, it opens the door to a thousand other opportunities.

When we talk about "a Power greater than ourselves," we have to be open to what that might be. It could be another person who is more expert in something than we are. It might even be an institution. The point is we can't find a solution that works until we give up on *our* "solutions" that aren't working.

When we surrender, God helps us find what we need, and frequently it is other people. As soon as I surrendered, I got the idea to go to the state hospital, and that's where I found the people who were used as a "power greater than myself" which could help restore me to sanity. That was the beginning for me right there.

Sometimes we struggle with wanting to *understand* a "Power greater than ourselves." There are many powers greater than ourselves that we don't understand. Electricity is a good example. We don't understand this power, but we use it constantly just by flipping a switch. One way we can come to believe is to *see* all the people around us whom God has changed.

One of these principles—one of the Steps—by itself is not effective. One of these principles by itself is of no value. We are talking about a set of principles, and they are all necessary. None of them, including belief, is effective by itself. These Steps interlock with each other. They are principles of success, principles of life.

Believing that a "Power greater than ourselves can restore us to sanity" is the cornerstone on which we are going to build our spiritual lives. When you hear that a new building is going to be built, and you go by after the cornerstone has been laid, you don't see much. It doesn't appear that much is there, but the beginning is there. It's the same way with us in our spiritual development. At first there isn't much to see, but this *coming to believe* is the very basis on which all the rest of our spiritual lives is built.

These Twelve Steps contain the principles of the way we change. Whatever you *believe,* you are going to *become,* good or bad. Whenever our lives are in a mess, we have been believing something that is untrue, and making decisions and taking actions based on untrue belief. We've been running headlong into a brick wall. That's why we've been having the problem in the first place. So what we have to do is believe differently. When we believe differently, we can decide differently, we can choose differently, we can act differently—we can become different.

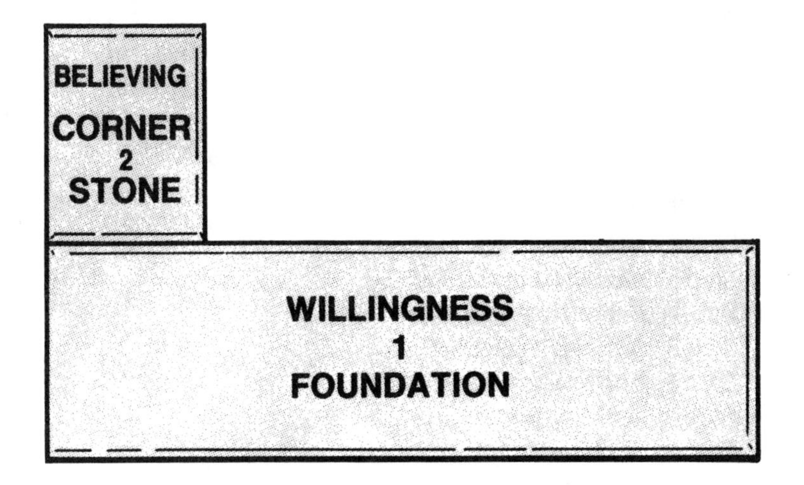

The Process of Spiritual Growth

Believing is the beginning of each thing that we accomplish in our lives. To be successful, believing must become strong enough to incite a decision, which is a choice of a course of action. Once this decision is made it has to become strong enough to incite action. Once the action becomes strong enough, it will bring about results. Once the results are plain and clear, we will have faith. Faith is true knowledge that comes as the result of action.

The Twelve Steps are based on this plan. These are the principles by which humankind has succeeded or failed.

The Twelve Steps:

Step 1: ***Willingness*** to change
Step 2: ***Believe*** we can change
Step 3: ***Decision*** to change
Step 4: ***Inventory*** to change
Step 5: ***Actions*** to change
Step 6: ***Actions*** to change
Step 7: ***Actions*** to change
Step 8: ***Actions*** to change
Step 9: ***Actions*** to change
Step 10: ***Actions*** to change
Step 11: ***Actions*** to change
Step 12: ***Changed***

We can now see that faith is knowledge that comes as a result of a complete process. This is why Step 12 is the conclusion, and we should not expect this result (faith) in Step 2. Many people fail because they are expecting true knowledge by faith before they make a decision to take any action and get results. We cannot begin with faith; we can only believe in the beginning. But this is all we need to get us started.

Adapted with permission
from *Recovery Dynamics*

Making a Decision

Our great trouble is that we are trying to make ourselves better. We can't really do that. We have to have God's help. We have to quit playing God because it hasn't worked. We have to make a decision that hereafter God is going to direct our lives.

Step 3: Made a decision to turn our will and our lives over to the care of God as we understood Him.

Each and every thing we do in our lives is based on a decision. Every action we take is preceded by a decision. Since our lives are action, then decision making is one of the most important principles for successful living.

Successful people are successful because of their ability to make decisions. Making decisions is simply gathering facts and determining a course of action based on interpretation of those facts as we perceive them. We don't know what the results of those decisions will be, but we do have certain pertinent information that we must gather. In this Twelve-Step process, the first two Steps have given us the information with which to make this decision. We have seen our alternatives, and we have a choice: we can choose to begin to live our lives on a spiritual basis. Step 3 is a principle that we should apply not only to our addiction or compulsion but to all areas of our lives as long as we live.

There may be a lot of variables in the quality of our decision making. For instance, many people make the mistake of not gathering all the information they need, and so make hasty decisions. They make bad decisions. Many people make a mistake by rounding up all the information but then—because they are afraid they'll make a mistake—waiting a long time to make sure they're ready. What can happen with these people is that some of the facts change, and they make the decision based on old information and get into trouble.

So, decision making is a little like rocket science: windows of opportunity occur which are dangerous to miss. Spacecraft have to be launched with precise timing, or they will miss their targets. It is likewise vital for us to make our decisions when they are timely—that is, after we have gathered enough information, but not after having waited timidly for so long that the opportunity has passed.

Step 1 and Step 2 have prepared us. We have gathered all the needed information through these two Steps. We are now ready for a decision. There is no need to procrastinate. Our window of opportunity is open.

The Big Book says on page 61,

> A life run on self-will can hardly be a success. On that basis we are almost always in collision with something or somebody, even though our motives are good. Most people try to live by self-propulsion. Each person is like an actor who wants to run the whole show; is forever trying to arrange the lights, the ballet, the scenery and the rest of the players in his own way.

What is "self-will"? This is a very important question. I think the key to being able to do an inventory in Step 4 is our ability to understand the meaning of *will* in Step 3. That's the heart of the inventory.

There are only two kinds of will on the face of this earth; in other words, there are only two forms of intelligence. These are *human will* (the will of men and women) and *the will of God.* No other animal or thing on earth has this will. We are the only animals who can think and make decisions; this is both our freedom and our curse.

There is a story in the Bible that tells how all this conflict began. The Garden of Eden story is the story of the beginning of self-will, and how we got it. In the beginning, when God created the earth, He made the sun, the trees, and the animals—who don't even know how to get into trouble. All these things were and are God-directed. God said since He had made these things, He would care for them. But God got lonesome in this kind of world. He wanted something else, something with will, something with intelligence. He decided to make human beings. He gave us intelligence so He would have something else in this whole scheme that was like Him, someone he could communicate with. The Bible says we are "God-like." We probably don't look like God, but we are "God-like" because we have will.

So He created Adam and Eve and put them in Serenity Park. It was a great place; they had it made. They were living there with a lot of dumb animals, and they were new at living and didn't know anything about self-will. God ran the whole show. The rest of the animals went along with the program, so Adam and Eve did, too. They didn't know any better and everything was going along just fine. They didn't use self-will; they didn't know anything about it.

One day the snake came up to Eve and he said, "Hey, Eve, what are you and Adam going along with this for? You've got self-will! You don't have to be just like all these dumb animals."

Eve had never heard such a thing. She said, "What's that?" So the snake ran it down to her. He said, "You can do whatever you want to! You don't have to listen to Him!"

Eve said, "Well, I didn't know that."

He said, "Yeah, you got it. I have to go along with this stuff, but you don't."

She couldn't wait. She ran to tell Adam. "Adam, Adam! We've got self-will!" He probably said, "What in the world is that?" So she explained it to him.

"You mean we can eat that apple?" he said.

"Yeah," she said, "we can do anything we want to do."

And Adam made a decision to eat the apple. It was a bad decision, but remember, it was the first decision he had ever made. So they ate the apple.

When God came along, He probably said, "Uh-oh, they've found out about it. They know what they've got." He wasn't surprised, but He kicked them out of the garden.

"Because," He told them, "if you are going to direct your own lives, exercise self-will, and make your own decisions, you're going to have to take care of yourselves. But if you get into trouble directing your own lives and want to turn your wills and your lives back over to me, let me know, and I'll take care of you again. It's up to you. I won't take your will away from you. You'll have to surrender it to me of your own choice."

Bill Wilson defined self-will very well when he wrote about it in *Twelve Steps and Twelve Traditions*. (See the beginning of the discussion of Step 4 in the *Twelve and Twelve.*) Bill talks about how nature gave us, as the highest order, three basic instincts of life that separate us from the lower animals.

SOCIAL INSTINCT

Companionship — Wanting to belong or be accepted.

Prestige — Wanting to be recognized, or to be accepted as a leader.

Self-Esteem — What we think of ourselves, high or low.

Pride — An excessive or unjustified opinion of oneself, either positive (self-love) or negative (self-hate).

Personal Relationships — Our relations with other human beings and the world around us.

Ambitions — Our palns to gain acceptance, power, recognition, prestige, etc.

We have a certain basic *social instinct.* We have a desire for companionship. We need prestige, or recognition by others. We need self-esteem. These things are part of our lives. They are instincts that allow us to survive. If we didn't feel a need for companionship, we wouldn't come together to cooperate. We couldn't accomplish much. Our companionship instincts are natural and necessary to our survival.

SECURITY INSTINCT

Material — Wanting money, buildings, property, clothing, etc., in order to be secure in the future.

Emotional — Based upon our needs for another person or persons. Some tend to dominate, some are overly dependent on others.

Ambitions — Our plans to gain material wealth, or to dominate, or to depend on others.

Another set of basic instincts that Bill talks about is our *security instincts.* These are of two kinds: material and emotional. If it weren't for our basic need for security, we wouldn't plant and harvest crops, and we wouldn't construct shelter. The human race would die out.

SEX INSTINCT

Acceptable — Our sex lives as accepted by society, God's principles or our own principles.

Hidden — Our sex lives that are contrary to either society, God's principles or our own principles.

Ambition — Our plans regarding our sex lives, either acceptable or hidden.

Bill also talks about a third basic instinct: the *sex instinct.* This instinct brings about reproduction, and keeps the human race going.

These three basic instincts go together to make up what we refer to as "self-will." Bill says, "So these desires—for the sex relation, for material and emotional security, and for companionship—are perfectly necessary and right, and surely God-given. Yet these instincts, so necessary for our existences, often far exceed their proper functions." (*Twelve and Twelve,* p.42) That is, they get out of control, and these God-given and necessary instincts become destructive.

If I think somebody or something is threatening one of my instincts (my need for prestige or self-esteem, or my material or emotional security, or my sex life), I become fearful and resentful, and this blocks me off from God. Most of our troubles stem from spiritual sickness; and this *spiritual sickness is nothing more or less than being blocked off from God by some fear, resentment, guilt, or remorse caused by self-will.*

Some people maintain that God punishes us when we do

BASIC INSTINCTS OF LIFE WHICH CREATE SELF

SOCIAL INSTINCT

Companionship — Wanting to belong or be accepted.

Prestige — Wanting to be recognized, or to be accepted as a leader.

Self-Esteem — What we think of ourselves, high or low.

Pride — An excessive or unjustified opinion of oneself, either positive (self-love) or negative (self-hate).

Personal Relationships — Our relations with other human beings and the world around us.

Ambitions — Our plans to gain acceptance, power, recognition, prestige, etc.

RESENTMENTS

Feelings of bitter hurt or indignation which come from rightly or wrongly held feelings of being injured or offended.

SECURITY INSTINCT

Material — Wanting money, buildings, property, clothing, etc., in order to be secure in the future.

Emotional — Based upon our needs for another person or persons. Some tend to dominate, some are overly dependent on others.

Ambitions — Our plans to gain material wealth, or to dominate, or to depend on others.

SEX INSTINCT

Acceptable — Our sex lives as accepted by society, God's principles or our own principles.

Hidden — Our sex lives that are contrary to either society, God's principles or our own principles.

Ambition — Our plans regarding our sex lives, either acceptable or hidden.

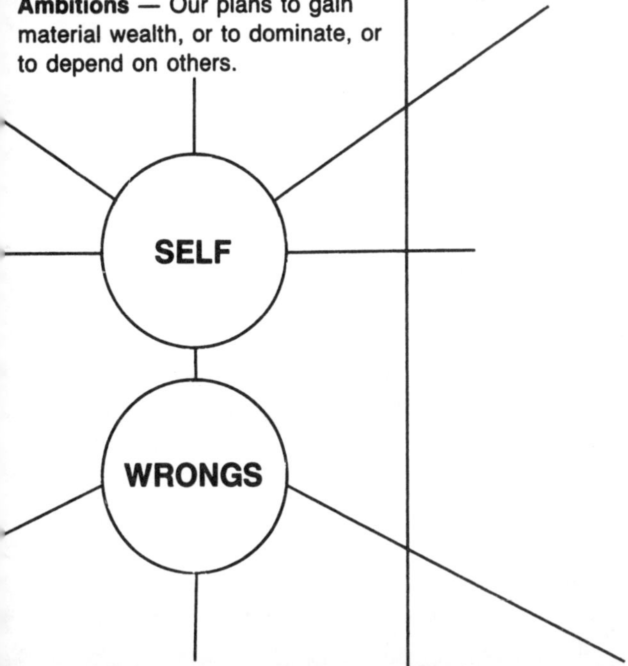

SELF

WRONGS

FEAR

Feelings of anxiety, agitation, uneasiness, apprehension, etc.

HARMS OR HURTS

Wrong acts that result in pain, hurt feelings, worry, financial loss, etc., for others and also self.

wrong, but He doesn't have to punish us. When we live our lives guided by self-will, we punish ourselves. This makes self-will sound like a curse, but we were given it for a certain purpose. All through this discussion, we will be talking about "faults," "character defects," and a lot of other things we refer to in negative terms. We need to remember that *all of them* are based on instincts vitally necessary to us. These instincts are not bad in themselves, but just when they're out of proportion or misused.

This is the case with self-will. Self-will is necessary. Our instincts keep us alive. Our instincts provide the drive which sets us apart from the lower animals and which has enabled us to make all the progress we have made.

But Bill says we are extreme examples of "self-will run riot," and we either rid ourselves of this selfishness, or it kills us. (Big Book, p. 62)

The destruction in our world, such as war, crime, and other human violence, is the result of the will of men and women. The destructive force in just one person's life can affect the world. For example, the Second World War resulted in the loss of millions of lives essentially because of the will of one man—Adolph Hitler. In fact, all of our human laws are written against self-will because if each person were allowed to freely satisfy his or her own will, chaos would exist. There would be no order, and thus no society. Just imagine our streets if anyone could drive on either side, at any speed, ignoring signs and stoplights, and so on!

But it seems there is no way we can overcome self-will without God's help. This principle is very simple: if we realize that there are only two wills on earth, human will and God's will, then self-will can only be overcome by God's will. *Self-will cannot overcome self-will.*

Our great trouble is that we are trying to make ourselves better. We can't really do that. We have to have God's help. We have to quit playing God because it hasn't worked. We have to *make a decision that hereafter God is going to direct our lives.*

At this point in the Big Book, Bill calls the willingness to turn our will and our lives over to the care of God the "keystone." Earlier he has referred to willingness as the "foundation," and

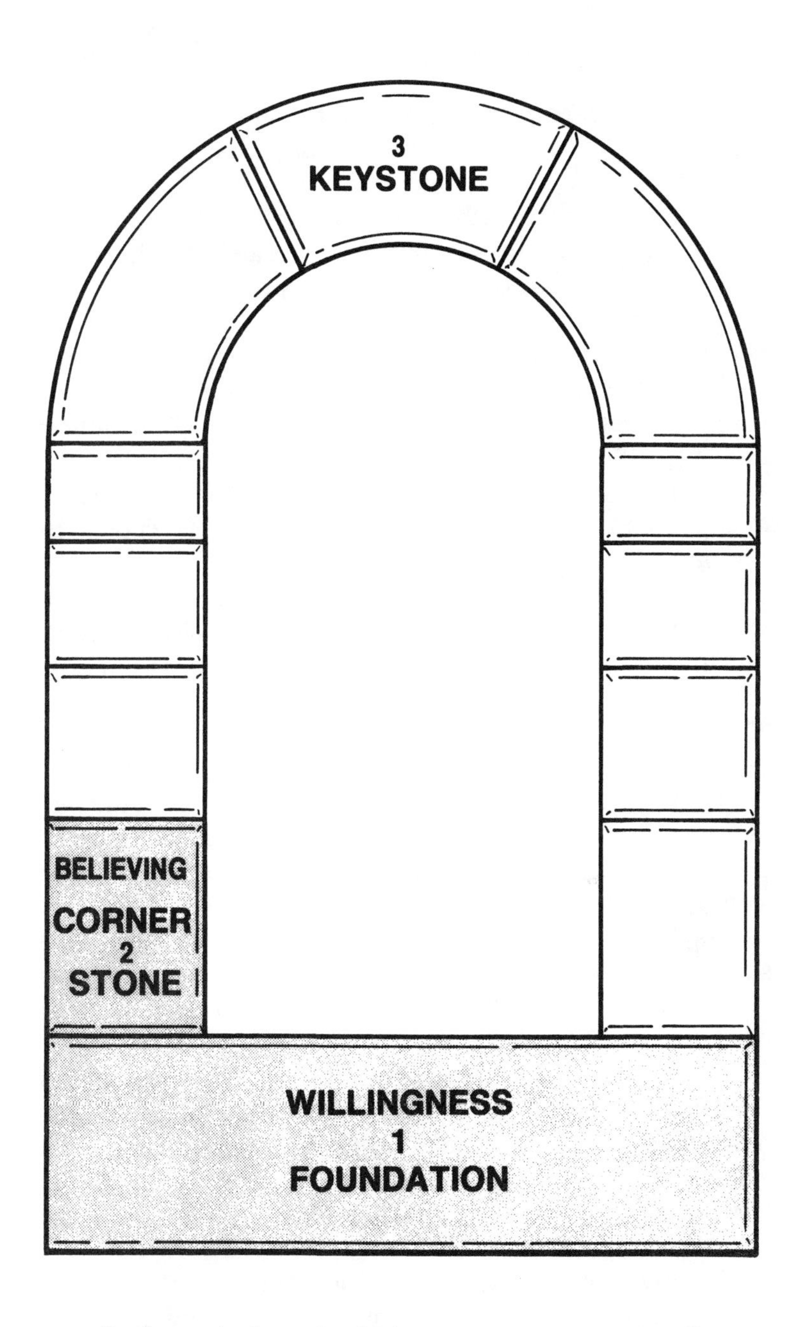

"...the arch through which we passed to freedom."

believing as the "cornerstone." He has been using these architectural terms, but so far we haven't realized what we were building. Now he says this surrender of our lives and our wills is the "...keystone of the arch through which we passed to freedom." (p. 62) Some people think turning your will and your life over to God is a trap, but it's not. It's an exit, a way out.

Sometimes it is desirable to take this Step with other people—the early people in AA and members of the Oxford Group took this Step together—but, as Bill Wilson wrote, "...it is better to meet God alone than with one who might misunderstand." (p. 63)

We need to remind ourselves here, too, that this is only a decision, and it must be followed *immediately* by action. The action is Step 4.

A friend of mine likes to tell this joke (I do, too): Three frogs were sitting on a log and one of them made a decision to jump into the pond. How many frogs were left on the log? Somebody will almost always shout, "Two!" My friend will say, "Nope. There were still three. He just made the *decision* to jump. He didn't *do* anything yet."

Of course, if I could turn my will and my life over to the care of God at Step 3, I wouldn't need to take any more Steps; I'd be perfect. But Step 3 says, "...made a *decision*..." It is just a decision, a beginning.

At this point in our restoration to sanity we have done something very important: we have laid the foundation and put the keystone in the arch. But we must not stop here. We must begin to take action now with Step 4.

Here's another example that emphasizes the importance of following through on the decision with action: If we decide to have a savings account at the bank, how much money will we be able to withdraw at the end of a year? None. To be able to withdraw money, we would have to open the account and make deposits. Once again, we only decided—we took no action.

We say that we have decided to turn our will and our lives over. This means our thoughts and our actions, too. Here is what a life is at any given moment: the sum total of all our actions.

OUR WILL = OUR THINKING

OUR LIVES = OUR ACTIONS

SO, WE TURN OVER OUR THINKING AND OUR ACTIONS

Actions follow decisions. God is within each person, and I believe we already know—maybe not clearly—but we already know how we should be living. Self-will is really a dominant thing, but deep down inside each of us we know how to live. We just have to get the other stuff out of the way.

We are rewarded or penalized according to our actions. Society puts people into prison not because of what they think, but because of what they do. You can think anything you want to. The theory goes that if society confines a person whose actions we don't consider acceptable, we will change his thinking. In most cases that doesn't work—because a person comes out of prison with *the same thinking he went in with.* He usually repeats the unacceptable actions, and we put him right back in. Unless his will changes, his actions can't change.

A person's actions are a manifestation of his thinking, his will. If some part of his will is out of control, he is going to behave in an unacceptable manner. Maybe his security instinct is out of balance; this could cause him to steal. Until this part of self is nurtured and straightened out, he will always go back to jail. Self is the root of his problem. At least one of the natural and useful instincts is out of balance.

We need always to remember that what causes our problems, what makes us criminal or simply miserable, is "self-will run riot." And the spiritual principle that is the cure is *surrender.*

When Bill said, "...made a decision to turn our will and our lives over to the care of God as we understood Him," he was trying to dress the idea up and make it more acceptable. But the cold, hard truth is that what we're talking about is surrender. *Surrender means giving up; it means you don't have to fight anymore.* It's all over. You don't have to run the show anymore.

My sponsor told me a story one time that applies here. He said when he was a young man, he used to box in these little gyms, and one of the things he'd do was go to small towns and box on Saturday nights. He said one of the biggest crowd pleasers, and a way to make some extra money, was the "free-for-all." Anybody in the audience could come up, put on gloves, and get in the ring—ten or twelve guys sometimes—and they would slug until only one was left standing. The fight organizers would have taken up a "pot" at the door—sometimes it would be fifteen or twenty dollars—and the last man standing got the pot. After a while people got smart, and started working in teams. Two or three guys would beat up all the other guys. Then all but one of them would lie down, and they'd split the pot.

But one night there was this young guy in there, and he was fighting two or three of them, and he was the last one in the ring who wasn't part of the set-up. He'd get knocked down, and as fast as he'd stand back up, they'd knock him down again. Well, he lasted a long time, but finally he was hanging on to the ropes and he said to my sponsor, "How do you get out of here?"

My sponsor said, "Just stay down. The next time you go down just don't get back up."

About turning our will and our lives over to the care of God—we would be better off if we could do this once and for all, but we can't. If a person is one hundred percent self-directed, becoming even *five* percent God-directed would mean a better life, maybe a pretty good life. He would probably be able to overcome the problems he's been facing. Most people think they need to go from one hundred percent self-directed to one hundred percent God-directed overnight! Of course, we can't do this—we're working on "spiritual progress rather than spiritual perfection." (Big Book, p. 60) Our self-will is ours until we die, and it seems we have to take it back from time to time. We have title to it. But we work to turn it over to the care of God.

How do we know if we are doing God's will or our own will? It's not always easy to tell. Some things are suspicious-looking. I may be doing something that I'm going to profit from and I'll wonder, "Am I doing this to promote myself, or is it God's will?" The Bible says that the workman is worthy of his hire. But I think you can *ask whether something you want to do is going to hurt another person.* Of course, it may not be God's will even if it isn't, but if it's going to hurt another, I don't think it *can* be God's will. This is one pretty good indicator.

Let me emphasize that we can't ever get entirely rid of self, because in its proper proportion it is necessary. Without self, we wouldn't care enough to get up and go to work in the morning; we wouldn't take a shower; we'd be a mess. Self esteem—we need it, but it gets out of control. Security—we have to have it, too. We have to worry enough about security to provide an adequate amount of it for ourselves. We are trying to find a balance in these things. *God will give us directions to find that balance if we surrender our lives and wills to His care.*

Now, as we make this decision, our God-concept will begin to grow. A person's concept of God is just as unique as his fingerprint. It's like everybody who goes to a football game sits in a different seat with a different angle to the action. Consequently, they each see a different game.

We each have a unique understanding of everything. I think the idea that we can turn ourselves over to the care of God "as we understand Him" opens the whole thing up, and makes it possible for everybody to get a concept of God.

At the beginning in AA, there were people who wanted a "narrow door," but they didn't win out, and this continued as a spiritual program, not a religious one. If you want to join up with most religious groups, you have to accept God as others—the authorities of that particular religious group—understand Him. But in Twelve-Step programs, we think it has to be up to the individual, because we think this is the only way that human beings really know anything.

In Step 2 we didn't have to believe everything. We didn't have to believe exactly what someone else believed. We only had to believe that a Power greater than ourselves (in whatever way we understood that Power) could help us. And in Step 3 we make a decision to turn our will and our lives over to the care of that Power. We don't have to accept some other person's or some group's definition; the Power is God *as we understand Him.*

I think there are a lot of people who have had trouble

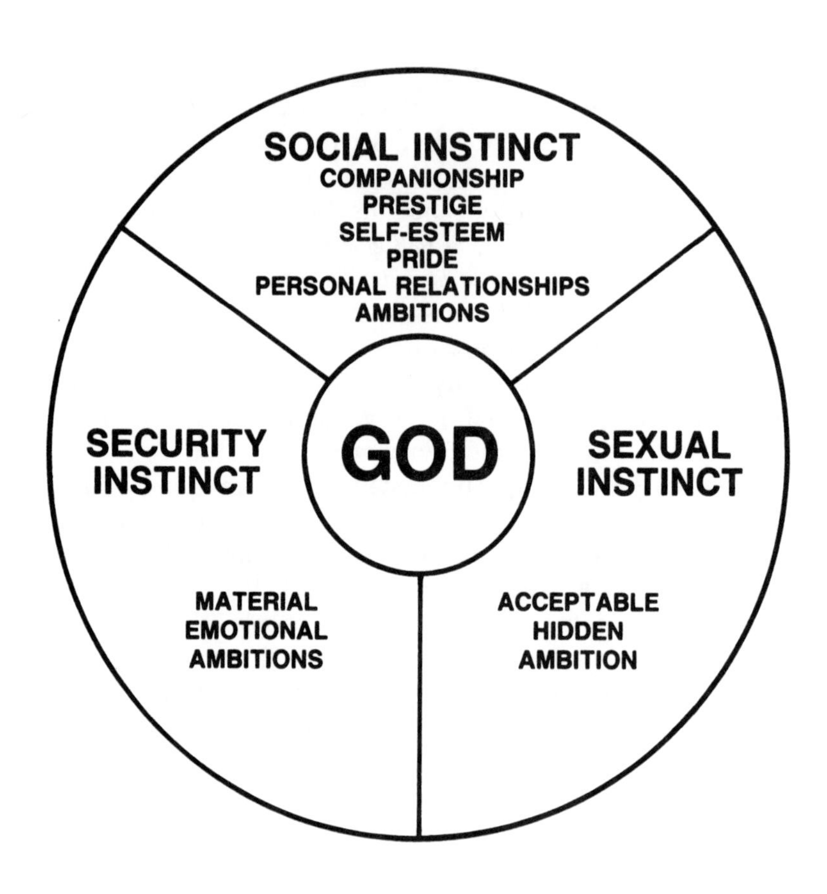
SOCIAL INSTINCT
COMPANIONSHIP
PRESTIGE
SELF-ESTEEM
PRIDE
PERSONAL RELATIONSHIPS
AMBITIONS
SECURITY INSTINCT
GOD
SEXUAL INSTINCT
MATERIAL
EMOTIONAL
AMBITIONS
ACCEPTABLE
HIDDEN
AMBITION

finding God because they have not been allowed to use their own understanding of God. They have felt forced to accept someone else's concept. A lot of well-meaning people say, "This is the concept of God that works for me, so you have to believe the same way." But, for example, the concept of God I have today is different from the concept I started with. I *couldn't* have started where I am now. I had to start where I was then. So does everyone.

Some people with a certain life experience have said, like David said in the 23rd Psalm, "The Lord is my shepherd." Others with different life experiences have said, "He is the captain of my ship." My own early concept, because I was living on the street like I was, was that God was my "partner." I couldn't even use the word "God." I bristled when I heard that word. I had some resistance; I just called him my "partner." As I look back on it, I realize it didn't take long for my concepts to broaden, but at first I had to start where I could. My old ideas of God (from religion, I suppose) were that He was something that looked down on me and watched me and punished me.

God's will is not totally absent from anybody. Sometimes we have obscured it so that we couldn't recognize it or didn't know it for what it was, but *we have always known God's will existed.* We've always known the destructive behavior we were carrying out was not right. We've always known some things were wrong, and some things were not God's will. Even while we were living on self-will, we knew that God's will was available, that goodness was available. We are talking about making a decision to awaken the goodness, the rightness we have always known was available to us when we chose to accept it.

When we are living on self-will, we know there is a right, good way to live, but we still choose to live unhappily on self-will. The knowledge of God's will is there from our creation, and now it's a matter of whether we are going to let it direct our lives.

When we are new in this program, we see that we have a choice: we can continue to live as we have been (we know that this is not good), or we can "believe" that a Power greater than ourselves (which we don't yet know anything about) can restore us to sanity. From Step 1 we've learned that we have been on a destructive course, and from Step 2 we've gotten the hope to believe there is a better way. Once we've looked at the choice that Steps 1 and 2 represent, once we've learned from experience the good results of letting God's will run our lives, we begin to know that we have made the right choice.

At the point of decision, it may seem to us that we are giving up something really valuable, but a few years later after we have had some experience living by God's will, we begin to realize that what we gave up was the worst thing in our lives. At the point of making the decision, it may seem to be too high a price to pay. But after a while we find that we seldom are interested in self-will and where it leads us.

We do well to recall that there are only two wills on earth: God's will and self-will, and self-will can only be overcome by God's will. *Self-will cannot overcome self-will.* That is our greatest trouble: we are trying to make ourselves better. We can't do it.

We can use these Steps for continuous renewal. Self-will is going to be with us for the rest of our lives. So we have to turn our wills and our lives over to the care of God every day for the rest of our lives, and the more we surrender, the better our quality of life will be.

Finally, we need to remember that this Step is but a decision. A lot of people think Step 3 says we turn our will and our lives over to the care of God. But Step 3 is only a decision; unless we take certain actions, the change we want in our lives will not happen. These actions are spelled out in the next Steps. We have decided that we want God to be the director of our lives, and now we have to set about taking the Steps that will remove the things that are blocking us from God.

Identifying What Blocks Us From God

Although the inventory is sometimes confusing to people, Bill offers us a brilliantly simple process in the Big Book. He explains how the things that blocked us from God manifested themselves in three major ways: resentments, fears, and harms done to others. He directs us to inventory and analyze these things.

Step 4: Made a searching and fearless moral inventory of ourselves.

The Big Book says that Step 3 has no permanent effect unless we follow it at once by removing the things that block us from God. (p. 64) Steps 3 and 4 are in sequence because these things have to be done in this order.

First, we have to realize that self-will has been blocking us from God's will. Then, we have to make a decision to turn our will over to the care of God, replacing that self-will with God's will. In order to do this, we have to identify the manifestations of self-will so we can start to eliminate them.

Step 4 is simply looking at those manifestations of self-will and identifying them, so that later on, in Step 5, we can talk them over with another person and learn more about them. Then in Step 6 we become willing to let go of them, and in Step 7 we are going to ask God to remove them.

So you see, these Steps are *actions* that will carry out the decision that we made in Step 3. *The results of Step 3 will not be based on the decision itself, but on the actions we take as a result of that decision.* So while Step 3 is a vital and crucial step, it has no permanent effect unless we follow it with actions, beginning with Step 4.

I believe Step 4 is a simple step if we follow the illustrated plan on pages 64 and 65 in the Big Book. The instructions are condensed and are sometimes difficult for a reader to understand and follow. There has been a lot of confusion about the process of taking an inventory, but it is really quite simple.

Bill Wilson starts off with a comparison, as he liked to do. He makes a parallel between the idea he is trying to get across and an example he thinks many people will easily understand. In this case, he chooses a business inventory to illustrate the process of personal inventory.

He asks us to consider ourselves the most important business on earth and to apply the inventory principles that a smart business person would apply to his or her business. A business that didn't know what it had to sell, or what it needed, wouldn't be able to meet the needs of its customers; the business person would have a lot of stuff he couldn't sell taking up shelf space, and he'd have a lot of money he was paying interest on that wasn't doing him any good. He would soon go broke.

Bill asks us to take *a written inventory,* to make a written list of items. This written list is a necessity because our life is a very complex thing, and there are a lot of parts to look at. If we don't write things down as we go through, we won't be able to retain the information we need, in the way we need to see it. I want to stress that an inventory is a written list of items. *There is no such thing as a mental inventory.* If you don't go to the trouble to write it down, you haven't taken an inventory.

Business Inventory	Personal Inventory
fact-finding	searching
fact-facing	fearless
truthful	moral

This Step uses the words "searching," "fearless," and "moral" to describe our personal inventory. When Bill says "searching," he means the same thing as "fact-finding." When he says "fearless," he means the same thing as "fact-facing." When he says "moral," he just means "true." So, we are going to make a *fact-finding, fact-facing, truthful,* written inventory of our personal "stock-in-trade," just as we would if we were inventorying a business that we wanted to run profitably. Our selves are the stock-in-trade.

If we look at ourselves as we would a business, we will see, I think, that what we have to "trade" in—to *deal* in—every day is our thoughts. "As a man thinketh, so he is." (Proverbs 23:7) That is, we are the sum total of the thoughts that go through our minds each day. So we want to inventory those thoughts and evaluate them. Then we can get rid of the "unsalable" goods, the thoughts that are making our lives unmanageable, and replace them with stock that will bring us a better return.

Although the inventory is sometimes confusing to people, Bill offers us a brilliantly simple process. He explains how the things that blocked us from God manifested themselves in three major ways: resentments, fears, and harms done to others. (Big Book, pp. 64-68) He directs us to inventory and analyze these things.

Number one for a selfish, self-centered person is *resentments.* Resentments effectively block us from God. At the time we have resentments, these thoughts dominate our minds, causing us to turn our lives over to the people and things we resent. If people and things we resent are directing our lives, we can't carry out the decision that we just made in Step 3.

The same is true for *fears* and *harms done to others.* I think it's important that we understand how these things control our minds. When we have fear, the fear dominates our mind; when we have harmed others, the guilt and remorse we feel for those actions turn our lives over to other people.

These are the three major areas of our lives that we need to look at. Most of our negative concerns from day to day can be placed under one of these headings. We are either mad about something, or we are afraid of something or someone, or we have done something for which we feel ashamed or remorseful. These are the three things we have to look at, to inventory.

We list and analyze them—these resentments, fears, and harms done to others—so we can see where they originated (Step 4), and so we can talk about them with another human being (Step 5), and so we can be willing to let them go (Steps 6 and 7).

A person who has been motivated by self-will has been making wrong judgments—resulting in resentments. He has been practicing wrong believing—resulting in fear. And he has taken, because of his fear and resentments, wrong actions—resulting in harms to others. I use an inclusive interpretation of the word *wrong*. It is important that we look at wrongs in this broader sense, so our definition doesn't include only wrong actions but also wrong judgment and wrong believing.

wrong judgments = resentments
wrong believing = fears
wrong actions = harms done to others

What we are going to do is look at these wrongs and analyze them. Here "analyze" means to get to the root cause, to the truth.

A resentment is a wrong because it blocks you from God, but it isn't what really started it. In Step 5, we talk about the "exact nature" of the resentment. Some people advise that it is good to vent feelings and to let resentments out, but unless we get to the root cause of the resentment, we have only made room for the *next* resentment to come in by expressing ourselves. This kind of venting may make us feel good for a while, but if we don't get to the cause of the wrong judgment, we will soon have another resentment to take that one's place, *and* the one we just expressed will usually still be there!

We say that the human mind cannot retain more than one predominant thought at a time. So as we do this inventory, we are going to look at one part at a time and *write it down*. Now our minds are free to search for the other parts. If we follow Bill W.'s system, when we're finished we'll have all the information we need to see the total picture at one time. And for the first time, we will be able to see the truth. *If we can see the truth about our resentments, we won't have them anymore.*

We are hunting for and analyzing the truth. We are like detectives at a crime scene: we have to go over the evidence at the scene, try to put the physical evidence together, analyze it, and see if we can tell what we have.

With a resentment, for example: the "crime" in this case, the wrong, is the resentment. And we want to get to the cause of the resentment. The "evidence" is the name of the person that we have a resentment toward. The most visible thing we can see, the most vivid thing, is the name of the person who offended us. So we start by listing the person's name.

We keep our minds on this predominant thought: we list all the names of people—or institutions or principles—for whom we have resentments. We make this list before we add anything about what the resentment is. We write just the names of all the people or things we have resentments against—left column, top to bottom, one thing at a time, *just the names.* We can remember these. We exhaust all of the resentments we have, identifying them by the names of people.

A mistake a lot of people make here is trying to list a person's name, then going right across the page to the next columns, and analyzing the resentment. But this means we have to change our minds four times as we list each resentment, to think about four different things about each resentment. This inevitably leads to confusion. It is better to name everyone and everything that we resent first, just thinking about one resentment at a time, working from top to bottom of this column. *Then* we move over and start the next column. [Look at the sample inventory forms included with this chapter to *see* how these instructions apply.]

So it's simple. We ask first, "Who are the people and things that I resent?" When we've finished making this list, we go on to the next column, and to the next most vivid thing in our memory, "What did he or she or it do to me?" We don't usually have any trouble remembering this either! Beside each name, in the second column, we put down the cause associated with that person or thing. These are very vivid; everyone readily remembers them. Some of them we have been replaying in our minds for years and years. We know what they are. We put all these down from top to bottom.

Now we have two columns. It's very interesting how the first column is the foundation. Once we get the name, from the name we extract the cause, and so the first column gives us the second column. Once we find the cause, we can trace directly to

Review Of

INSTRUCTIONS FOR COMPLETION

Instruction 1 — In dealing with resentments we set them on paper. We listed people, institutions, or principles with whom we are angry. (Complete column 1 from top to bottom. Do nothing on columns 2, 3, or 4 until column 1 is complete.)

Instruction 2 — We asked ourselves why we were angry. (Complete column 2 from top to bottom. Do nothing on columns 3 or 4 until column 2 is complete.)

Instruction 3 — On our grudge list we set opposite each name our injuries. Was it our self-esteem, our security, our ambitions, our personal or sex relations which had been interfered with? (Complete each column within column 3 going from top to bottom, starting with the Self-Esteem column and finishing with the Sexual Ambitions column. Do nothing on column 4 until column 3 is complete.)

Instruction 4 — (Referring to our list again.) Putting out of our minds the wrongs others had done, we resolutely looked for our own mistakes. Where had we been selfish, dishonest, self-seeking, and frightened and inconsiderate? (Asking ourselves the above questions, we complete each column within column 4.)

Instruction 5 — Reading from left to right we now see the resentment (column 1), the cause (column 2), the part of self that had been affected (column 3), and the exact nature of the defect within us that allowed the resentment to surface and block us off from God's will (column 4).

	COLUMN 1	COLUMN 2
	I'm resentful at:	The cause:
1		
2		
3		
4		
5		
6		
7		

Resentments

"SELF" COLUMN 3									COLUMN 4			
Affects My... (Which part of self caused the fear?)									What is the exact nature of my wrongs, faults, mistakes, defects, shortcomings:			
Social Instinct		Security Instinct		Sex Instinct		Ambitions						
Self-Esteem	Personal Relationships	Material	Emotional	Acceptable Sex Relations	Hidden Sex Relations	Social	Security	Sexual	Selfish	Dishonest	Self-Seeking Frightened	Incnsiderate

the part of self that was threatened, and so the second column gives us the third column. Once we know which instinct felt threatened, then we can look at the *real* information we need: the "exact nature" of the resentment.

We will be able to see what we have done, how we have been involved, what part of our character (what "character defect") was associated with the particular resentment. (See Appendix 3, Self-Pity.) Often we will find that *we have said or done something* that caused the other person to react in the way he or she did that caused our resentment. The Big Book says we have often done something based on self that struck these people, and they retaliated against us. (p. 62) Usually we will be able to see it right away. Now we can really get down to the basics because *the important thing is the fourth column.*

If we go back and look at our columns, we see that Column 1 is just where we began, and it isn't very important because we can't change what that person did. We need to change the third column, but we can't. Only God can overcome the self. What we *can* go to work on is that stuff in the fourth column. All the vital information appears in the fourth column.

Whether we're looking at resentments, fears, or harms done to others, the roots are the same: dishonesty, lack of consideration, selfishness, self-seeking, and fear. But these weren't (in fact, *couldn't* be) immediately evident to us. We had to start from something we could see and work backward to the truth.

It is not by chance that we have resentments. Resentments (fear and sex, too) are useful tools. Without them we wouldn't be complete human beings. In some situations they are vitally necessary. It's like in the Bible, where it says there is a time for everything. (Ecclesiastes 3:1) At the right time, all these things are necessary. For instance, we might say that competition and resentment are related. Often I accomplish something I wouldn't otherwise accomplish, because of a feeling of resentment or competition with another person. A lot of the progress we have made has been because we were motivated by fear that somebody was getting ahead of us.

Thirty-some years ago, people in this country woke up and discovered that the Soviet Union was ahead of us in space science. They had Sputnik going around and around the earth. Well, out of a sense of resentment—or fear—or competition—we went to work and soon had men on the moon. We might still not have accomplished it without these feelings.

What we're doing here is not getting totally rid of anything, of any of these resentments or fears or harms done to others. The Big Book says we are *rearranging things into a proper perspective.* (See p. 27 about Dr. Carl Jung's advice.) We are going to adjust; we are going to put these things, these feelings, in their proper places—because they are sometimes useful to us when we use them properly. But we need to keep this in mind: as long as we are mentally replaying these resentments or fears or the guilt feelings from harms done to others, we are turning our lives over to others and allowing others to dominate us.

The work we do on Step 4 enables us to *begin to know and understand ourselves.* The inventory is part of a study, a *lifetime* study, of ourselves. When we know ourselves, we know where we're going and what we stand for and how we're going to be. Then, if someone says something we don't like, something that might have hurt our feelings before, it won't hurt now—because we know ourselves and we're not as vulnerable as we used to be.

INSANITY IS INABILITY TO SEE THE TRUTH.
SANITY IS ABILITY TO SEE THE TRUTH.
AN INVENTORY IS A TOOL TO ENABLE US TO SEE THE TRUTH.
THE TRUTH WILL SET US FREE.

Review

INSTRUCTIONS FOR COMPLETION

Instruction 1 — In dealing with fears we set them on paper. We listed people, institutions, or principles with whom we were fearful. (Complete column 1 from top to bottom. Do nothing on columns 2, 3, or 4 until column 1 is complete.)

Instruction 2 — We asked ourselves why we have the fear. (Complete column 2 from top to bottom. Do nothing on columns 3 or 4 until column 2 is complete.)

Instruction 3 — What part of self caused the fear? Was it our self-esteem, our security, our ambitions, our personal or sex relations which had been interfered with? (Complete each column within column 3 going from top to bottom, starting with the Self-Esteem column and finishing with the Sexual Ambitions column. Do nothing on column 4 until column 3 is complete.)

Instruction 4 — (Referring to our list again.) Putting out of our minds the wrongs others had done, we resolutely looked for our own mistakes. Where had we been selfish, dishonest, self-seeking, and frightened and inconsiderate? (Asking ourselves the above questions, we complete each column within column 4.)

Instruction 5 — Reading from left to right we now see the fear (column 1), why we have the fear (column 2), the part of self that caused the fear (column 3), and the exact nature of the defect within us that allowed the fear to surface and block us off from God's will (column 4).

	COLUMN 1	COLUMN 2
	I'm fearful of:	Why do I have the fear?
1		
2		
3		
4		
5		
6		
7		

Of Fears

"SELF" COLUMN 3									COLUMN 4			
Affects My... (Which part of self caused the fear?)									What is the exact nature of my wrongs, faults, mistakes, defects, shortcomings:			
Social Instinct		Security Instinct		Sex Instinct		Ambitions						
Self-Esteem	Personal Relationships	Material	Emotional	Acceptable Sex Relations	Hidden Sex Relations	Social	Security	Sexual	Selfish	Dishonest	Self-Seeking Frightened	Incnsiderate

Review Of Ou

INSTRUCTIONS FOR COMPLETION

Instruction 1 — We listed people we harmed. (Complete column 1 from top to bottom. Do nothing on columns 2, 3, or 4 until column 1 is complete.)

Instruction 2 — We asked ourselves what we did. (Complete column 2 from top to bottom. Do nothing on columns 3 or 4 until column 2 is complete.)

Instruction 3 — Was it our self-esteem, our security, our ambitions, our personal or sex relations which had been interfered with? (Complete each column within column 3 going from top to bottom, starting with the Self-Esteem column and finishing with the Sexual Ambitions column. Do nothing on column 4 until column 3 is complete.)

Instruction 4 — (Referring to our list again.) Putting out of our minds the wrongs others had done, we resolutely looked for our own mistakes. Where had we been selfish, dishonest, self-seeking, and frightened and inconsiderate? (Asking ourselves the above questions, we complete each column within column 4.)

Instruction 5 — Reading from left to right we now see the harm (column 1), what we did (column 2), the part of self that caused the harm (column 3), and the exact nature of the defect within us that allowed the harm to surface and block us off from God's will (column 4).

	COLUMN 1	COLUMN 2
	Who did I harm?	What did I do?
1		
2		
3		
4		
5		
6		
7		

One of the deepest ways that people harm each other is through **sexual harms**, so these are the first form of harms we look at. (See the Big Book, pp.68-69). After we have completed the inventory of sexual harms, we then put down on another inventory form all the **other** ways we have harmed people — for example, if we have stolen from a person.

Sex Conduct

"SELF"
COLUMN 3

COLUMN 4

Affects My... (Which part of self caused the harm?)									What is the exact nature of my wrongs, faults, mistakes, defects, shortcomings:			
Social Instinct		Security Instinct		Sex Instinct		Ambitions						
Self-Esteem	Personal Relationships	Material	Emotional	Acceptable Sex Relations	Hidden Sex Relations	Social	Security	Sexual	Selfish	Dishonest	Self-Seeking Frightened	Incnsiderate

“Improving on” the Truth

I believe the happiest an individual is ever going to be is when he is in this pattern of living, relying on God and on other people. This is the design of life—to rely on God and others, as well as ourselves.

Step 5: Admitted to God, to ourselves, and to another human being the exact nature of our wrongs.

Step 5 is a subtle Step. In fact, we might easily assume the attitude that it could be avoided!

If we go back and examine the whole process of the Steps thus far, we can see that the goal of the process is to find the truth. The Bible talks about knowing God "in spirit and in truth." (John 4:24) Ultimately we may see God as the truth. The whole process of the Steps is built around this fact.

In the first Step, we understood the problem; we were looking for the truth, the true nature of the problem. Once we saw it, we came to believe in a Power greater than ourselves that would restore us to sanity, and that is the truth. In other words, we came to believe that truth exists. In Step 3, we made a decision to turn our lives over to the care of that truth. In order to act on that decision, we needed to find out what was blocking us from the truth, and we did that in Step 4.

The fifth Step is a further search for the same thing. In Step 5, we examine the information we found in Step 4 and make sure it is the truth. We try to "improve on" the truth we've found, to get a better quality of truth. Step 5 is an evaluation of the inventory in an attempt to get a better look at the information we gathered in the inventory process.

Why is this "improving on" Step 4's truth necessary?

If an individual has had a problem for weeks, months, or even years, and didn't know he had a problem, it's pretty obvious he is not an expert on the truth! After going through the first four Steps, we don't rely on the information as *we* see it. We don't have a good record of the truth. No one individual really knows the truth anyway—only God knows the truth. We human beings only have our perception of the truth. We can see now that before Step 1 our perception of the truth was very much distorted.

Thus we don't want to rely on our limited, perhaps distorted, opinion of what we found in the inventory. Step 5 is getting an outside viewpoint, a different look at things, from God, ourselves, and others.

It is interesting and not by chance that Step 5 is laid out in this way. The center of our lives is spiritual—our God—so the first thing we have to do is talk things over with God. The second dimension of our lives is ourselves—our minds—and so we look at things in this way. The third dimension is other people; therefore, finally, we talk with another person.

As we go through this, we talk to God about it. Even at this point we'll begin to get new insights. In the process of the Steps, we are trying to get to this consciousness with God. So we begin Step 5 by talking with God. Next we re-examine these things ourselves, and begin to see things we couldn't see before. The final part of the process, then, is to talk with another human being about it. We tell someone else who is not involved, not emotionally involved, in our lives. In most cases, he or she can easily see the real truth of the situation.

Getting someone else's viewpoint is important. You know, we all see things in a different light. For example, when an accident happens on the street, the police may question a person over there, one over here, and another over there. All saw the same accident; however, they each saw it differently. How they are emotionally involved affects the truth. It's very hard to find out what the truth is because we all look at things from different angles.

Today we are very blessed because in any community there are people who have been through this inventory and who are knowledgeable enough to sit down and do it with us. It is encouraging that the people who are completing it *now* will be the ones to help people in the future—but the Big Book says that all it has to be is an "understanding person" who is not involved, and who can look at our inventory as an outsider. The Big Book gives a whole page on choosing this person. (Big Book, p. 74) It says we might choose someone from our religion, a priest or minister, or maybe a psychiatrist or psychologist. It also suggests we can go to a trusted friend. Remember that when the Book was written in 1935 there wasn't anybody around who knew anything about sponsoring!

The main requirement we have is that we tell it to an outsider, because we have been very emotionally involved. We have conned ourselves with resentments. Even though we have been as honest as we can, we have taken the blame and transferred it from ourselves to another person. If we are an alcoholic or some other kind of sick person, we have developed these skills. Even if we've been as honest as we can, how honest *is* that at this point? We have to get someone to listen to us who is not emotionally involved. Basically, that's all this is: getting a second opinion.

After we have taken "inventory" in Step 4, and then have carried our inventory on through the process suggested in Step 5, we'll be surprised how much better information we have than if we'd stopped right when we completed the inventory. Talking to God, getting a new viewpoint in our own minds, then talking it over with another person—by doing these, we've improved on the information and taken a better look at things.

We look at resentments. We've found out they are a distortion of the truth—a way to take a situation, cast the blame on somebody else, and totally escape, so we have nothing to do with it whatsoever! A resentment is really a way of transferring blame. To accept a situation (to see ourselves and own our faults in it) is the best way to get through it, but to accept is painful.

Sometimes we push the pain away by transferring the blame to other people. By saying it was their fault, we are escaping and wiping our slate clean. But then we have to keep this lie up, and we begin to believe that it *is* the truth. It's the truth as far as we see it, but it's not the truth. So we do this for a period of time—months, maybe even years—blaming, using others as scapegoats, and then we don't really know what the truth is. In time, the lie of resentment has enslaved us. But the truth will set us free.

A lot of the time we use fear the same way. Many people say, "I *would* do that, but..." A fear is keeping them from doing something, and it really isn't true. If they could only see the truth, the fear, they could do whatever they wanted to do. But they have this fear of something and believe they can't do it. The truth is they have the ability to do anything they want to do.

For example, lots of people need to and want to go back to school and get an education. But many people who have been away from school for a period of time believe the lie that they can't compete with the other people in school. They have the ability to go back to school. They have the same minds, the same abilities, and maybe a little more initiative than they had when they were originally there—and often more initiative than people who *are* in school.

What keeps them from going back, what blocks them, is fear. Of course, that fear is a lie. But it's the truth to them. So they operate on the "truth," and they don't go back to school. If they could really see the truth, they could be free from that lie, and they could go back and do the things they want to. What we are searching for here is the ultimate truth, to improve on what we have found in Step 4.

I also think Step 5 puts the first crack in our armor. In the third part of Step 5—talking to another human being—we talk openly to someone else for the first time, and that gets us out of ourselves. The Big Book says, "We must be entirely honest with somebody if we expect to live long or happily in this world." (pp. 73-74)

We were designed to rely on God (the first part of Step 5) and on other people (the third part of Step 5), and we ourselves are in the middle. I believe the happiest an individual is ever going to be is when he or she is in this pattern of living, relying on God and on others. We who choose to live in this pattern have admitted that we have been selfish and self-seeking, that we have had the problem ourselves. We have wrestled with life on a "self" basis, cut ourselves off from God, and cut ourselves off from other people.

So we see that this Step is the first time we are really practicing a healthy way of living and fitting ourselves into a design of living that really works. *This is the design of life*—to rely on God and others as well as ourselves—regardless of whether we choose to live it or not. If we are to be more healthy, we must be in connection with God and with other people. This is not an easy thing for a selfish, self-seeking person to do—because he is used to relying on himself.

We have talked about the three levels of looking at the truth in Step 5, but what are we to discuss? What we are to discuss is often misunderstood. Step 5 is not a confession. Step 5 is not a *general* discussion. This is a very specific discussion that we do in Step 5.

Step 5 says we admit the "exact nature of our wrongs." It doesn't say we admit our wrongs. We can get bent out of shape when we think we have to discuss our wrongs. All people are defensive in this area. But our wrongs are not the focus of this Step. The focus of this Step is specifically stated as the "exact nature of our wrongs."

We have said that resentment is wrong judgment, fear is wrong believing, and harm to others is wrong action. These are the three basic things we analyzed in Step 4, and yet these resentments, fears, and harms themselves are not even what we are discussing in Step 5. Step 5 is still a little more in detail.

In Step 5, we ask "Where did these resentments, fears, and harms done to others originate?" The "exact nature" is the origin of these things, the inherent characteristic of these things. We have examined them as we went through the inventory process in Step 4. For example, with resentments, we found the exact nature of each resentment in the fourth column. (See inventory form in Step 4 or in Appendix 4.) In the first column we had the resentment; in the second, the cause; in the third, which basic instinct was affected. The first two columns we can't change. The third—our basic instincts that make up self—we have decided to turn over to the care of God since only God can correct self-will.

But we find in the fourth column the selfishness, self-seeking, dishonesty, fearfulness, and lack of consideration in our characters. (See the Big Book, pp. 67 and 69, for a list of these as our basic character defects.) As a result of one of these character defects, self has been out of control and allowed the whole thing to occur.

As we inventory the problem, we are looking at it from the outside in, but we want to remember that *the problem occurred from the inside out.* What we have done in the inventory (and what we are improving on in Step 5) is trace the problem from the outside, all the way in, to find the core of it—its exact nature.

> **What we are looking for is the "exact nature of our wrongs":**
> **Was I dishonest?**
> **Was I selfish?**
> **Was I self-seeking?**
> **Was I inconsiderate?**
> **Was I fearful?**

These problems actually developed from the inside outward, to be manifested finally in resentments, fears, and harms done to others. At the core of resentments, fears, and harms done to others is the exact nature of the problem, or its origin, in selfishness, self-seeking, dishonesty, fearfulness, or lack of consideration.

At least one of these has raised its head. If it had not, then the resentment (or fear or harm) would never have happened. Even if the person had done the same action to you, you would not have resented it if you hadn't had one of those character defects within your personality at the time. So the exact nature of all our wrongs, faults, defects, mistakes, shortcomings—whatever we choose to call them—is at the core of each resentment, fear, and harm done.

Step 4 and Step 5 are actually parts of the same process. One is putting it down, and the other is improving on it. Step 5 is fine-tuning the inventory. There is no way, if you really had all these problems, that you could see the truth by yourself. Even as well as you could see it, it would not be enough. I want to stress that to do the inventory *and not do Step 5 soon after* could be painful, even harmful. That's why Step 5 is right there, so we can raise the things we've seen in Step 4 on up to the surface and get them out.

When we have all our fears inventoried and analyzed, when we have all our resentments inventoried and analyzed, when we have all the sex conduct and other harms done to others listed and analyzed, then we are going to show it to that other human being. Then this other person can, because he or she is not emotionally involved, improve on the understanding we have of the information we've gathered.

What the person will do is this: He will look in the first column at the name of the person we resent (or the name of the fear, or the name of the harm we've done to another), and quite naturally there will be nothing he can do about any of them. He cannot improve on this information because it happened in the past and cannot be changed. He will look at the second column, and these things also happened in the past and there's no additional information here, either. But what he will begin to look at very closely is the third column.

Chances are there will be some things that were affected that we didn't really notice were affected. There might be some things in the third column that we thought were affected, but he doesn't agree. So there might be some changes—some improvement—we can make in the third column. By getting feedback from this person who was not involved we might see where something we had called "security instinct" was really something else, and we might see it in a more useful way.

Also, this other human being will maybe add or take away things from our fourth column. These are things about our character defects, and we want our information about them to be correct because this is what we are going to work on in Steps 6 and 7. We want to be correct about their exact nature, because the wrongs are *not* the resentments or the fears or the harms done to others—the *exact nature of the wrongs* is whether we were "frightened, self-seeking, selfish, inconsiderate, dishonest," and what was behind it, and where it originated.

These are the things we want to be sure about. All humans have these characteristics, and they are not things we are ever going to be perfectly rid of. But we've got to have specific knowledge of the degree of problems that we have in each of

Review C

INSTRUCTIONS FOR COMPLETION

Instruction 1 — In dealing with resentments we set them on paper. We listed people, institutions, or principles with whom we are angry. (Complete column 1 from top to bottom. Do nothing on columns 2, 3, or 4 until column 1 is complete.)

Instruction 2 — We asked ourselves why we were angry. (Complete column 2 from top to bottom. Do nothing on columns 3 or 4 until column 2 is complete.)

Instruction 3 — On our grudge list we set opposite each name our injuries. Was it our self-esteem, our security, our ambitions, our personal or sex relations which had been interfered with? (Complete each column within column 3 going from top to bottom, starting with the Self-Esteem column and finishing with the Sexual Ambitions column. Do nothing on column 4 until column 3 is complete.)

Instruction 4 — (Referring to our list again.) Putting out of our minds the wrongs others had done, we resolutely looked for our own mistakes. Where had we been selfish, dishonest, self-seeking, and frightened and inconsiderate? (Asking ourselves the above questions, we complete each column within column 4.)

Instruction 5 — Reading from left to right we now see the resentment (column 1), the cause (column 2), the part of self that had been affected (column 3), and the exact nature of the defect within us that allowed the rese ment to surface and block us off from God's will (column 4).

	COLUMN 1 I'm resentful at:	COLUMN 2 The cause:
1		
2		
3		
4		
5		
6		
7		
	We cannot change or control this column.	We cannot change this column — it is our past.

esentments

“SELF” COLUMN 3									THIS IS OUR BUSINESS! COLUMN 4			
Affects My... (Which part of self caused the fear?)									What is the exact nature of my wrongs, faults, mistakes, defects, shortcomings:			
Social Instinct		Security Instinct		Sex Instinct		Ambitions						
Self-Esteem	Personal Relationships	Material	Emotional	Acceptable Sex Relations	Hidden Sex Relations	Social	Security	Sexual	Selfish	Dishonest	Self-Seeking Frightened	Incnsiderate

We made a decision to turn this over to the care of God.

THIS IS OUR BUSINESS!

these areas. No two people are exactly alike, and they vary from one of us to another. I need to look down the columns and see patterns of problem areas that are *mine.* Maybe I have a lot of dishonesty; maybe I've got a lot of fear. I can work on these things that are mine. It doesn't do me much good to say, "Well, I'm just about like everyone else." I can't run my life off that.

So we're going to go through each inventory, and work all the way across to the fourth column and examine the exact nature of our wrongs. (You may choose to call them faults, defects, mistakes, shortcomings, or whatever you choose. These are different words for essentially the same thing). I need to see that the problem started *within me,* not with what "those other people" did. The things in the fourth column are what we are going to work on. Let's say it again: We can't do anything about other people (what's in Columns 1 and 2), either in the past or present or even in the future. We can't do much about self (what's in Column 3), except make a decision to turn the instincts that make up self over to God, and so that's God's business. *The only thing we can do is work on what's in Column 4.*

If we can get rid of these characteristics in the fourth column, chances are the self will be healthy. Some of the things we have inventoried were probably people retaliating against us. Some of the things *they* did were probably because of what *we* did in the first place. When we're not doing those things anymore—things based on selfish, dishonest, self-seeking, frightened, and inconsiderate character—there's not going to be a lot of retaliation.

Of course, every once in a while somebody will do something against us anyway. But still, if we're spiritually well, it won't make any difference. We won't have a barrage of stuff going on because we are healthy.

A resentment, fear, or harm may appear to be another person's problem, but it is really our problem. I think realizing this is freedom. If you really want to be free in your life, and you want to be happy, then the problems have to be your problems. As soon as you say, "*They* did it," then you're giving up your freedom. You are turning your life back over to the world again and enslaving yourself.

When I say, "I've got a problem," I say, "I sure hope it's mine." If it's mine, I have a chance to do something about it. If it's somebody else's problem, I can't do *anything* about it.

People usually associate freedom with political freedom, democracy, something like that. But the greatest freedom in the world is not that kind of freedom. It's the individual freedom God has given us as human beings. We are created as free people. I think when our forefathers wrote the Constitution, that's what they were reflecting. These were very spiritual people, and what they were saying was "this is the way we are all born."

We are born free, free from what anyone else does. And we give that up ourselves by buying into things, by giving other people resentments, and fearing *this*, and worrying about *that*, and developing these selfish, self-seeking parts of our character. And then we end up confined by alcohol or food or other people (or other compulsive behavior), and this all gets wrapped into a great big ball, a cobweb of emotional tangle.

We were created free, and we have done this job of tangling things up all by ourselves. And now we blame it on others. We have worked at it for years, winding ourselves up into this thing. Freedom takes work; freedom takes responsibility. When you say "this is my problem," you take responsibility. But it takes a little work, a little pain to admit that.

It's easier to transfer blame to someone else, and keep on going. But you're really stacking up something when you do that—it's like sweeping dirt under the carpet—and it's going to be worse later on when it comes out. And this is all resentment is; this is all fear is; this is all our guilt and remorse is.

Take guilt and remorse, for example. If we had made amends when the thing for which we feel guilty happened, we wouldn't have carried the guilt and remorse for twenty years. But we didn't do that, and the guilt and remorse got bigger and bigger and bigger, a bigger load to carry. If we had made amends when it first happened, we would have been free.

Freedom takes work. I always say one of the ways to be secure—emotionally secure in every way—is, ironically, to be a slave. A slave is taken care of, his master feeds him, gives him a

An example of "improving on the truth."

Let's be specific. One of the ways we harm people is through our sex conduct. Let's say we put down a person's name in column one, and we committed adultery in column two. We may have spent many hours as we've looked back over our lives feeling bad as a result of that incident. We've probably assumed that this harm was caused by our sex instinct, and we've probably listed it on our inventory this way.

But when another person looks at this, he is going to question us about it. A lot of times we're going to find out that the sexual harms we've done were caused by our social instincts, by trying to build our self-esteem. Or sometimes we have used sex to "buy" material security. We don't really care about it, but we feel we need this other person's material good for our survival. Sometimes our sexual harms are motivated by emotional security: we are just lonely. Very few times are they caused by our sex drive itself.

When another person helps us look at the harms we've done and see that we are really lonely—or financially insecure, or trying to build our self-esteem—then we have a better feeling about it. We know the exact nature of it. Maybe we can get a grip on it now. We can look over in the fourth column and see that if we weren't so frightened, or self-seeking, or inconsiderate we wouldn't have been thinking that way, and this would never have happened.

place to stay, tells him when to eat and what to eat, when to get up and when to go to bed. Of course, the slave has no freedom whatsoever. To be free, he would have to take care of himself, to do some things.

I think it's the same way in our emotional lives. When we don't do the daily things we need to do to live and be free, when we don't face things and deal with them, when we don't admit our faults, when we sweep things under the rug, then we give up our freedom. We are then in bondage, and this is manifested by, *expressed* by, all kinds of problems: alcoholism, drug dependency, co-dependency, and so on. If we've gotten into this state through many years of living, it will be difficult to do Step 5. Step 5 is thus a process of going back and clearing up those things that we've swept under the rug, and it's painful. It's not an easy thing for a person who has been living this way to start living the right way.

And then, of course, we have to keep it up. But we do it because we see the benefit, and we see the stupidity of the old way. For example, if you drove your car down the street and somebody said, "What's that noise?" and you said, "It ain't nothing; it's just the street," you're sweeping it under! Later, somebody else tells you, "I believe I hear a noise." You say, "Aw, it's nothing." And you keep on, and pretty soon parts of the car will be falling off. You see, it's painful to stop and admit something's wrong, and, of course, you have fear—fear of what it's going to cost you. Maybe if you had fixed it at first, the first day you heard the little noise, it wouldn't have cost so much. After months of trying to escape, you may find the car is ruined. You know the saying: "Pay me now or pay me later."

That's how it is with life: "Pay me now or pay me later." Do it *now* or pay more, maybe much more, later on.

This is what we're doing in Step 5. And, you know, although we want to have confidence in the person who hears our Step 5, and feel that he or she has "been there," there's really no great wisdom or insight necessary on his or her part. I remember someone came up to me and related a situation in great detail. And it was obvious to me as soon as I heard it what the problem was. I said, "This is your problem right here."

The person looked at me and said, "How did you know that?" "Well, you told me," I said.

"How could you see it so plainly?" the person asked.

And I answered, "I wasn't *involved* in it; you *were*."

We have to remember that we don't see too well. I always say I only see so far, and I only hear so far. I come home from work in the evenings, and I turn my television on to ABC or NBC or CBS. They can see farther than I can. I watch the 5:30 news and find out what's going on in Russia or China—beyond the limits of my sight. (That's relying on a power greater than myself.)

So we seek truth. Step 5 is a very rewarding Step. We do not know the results of a Step until after it's taken. In Step 5, the decision of Step 3 and the effort and honesty of Step 4 become meaningful because we begin to get some results. Personality change begins as a result of Step 5.

As our quality of life gets better and better, some of the things we used to live with will become objectionable, and we'll get rid of those. As we continue to grow, we say, "Well, I used to live with that, but I can't anymore."

Change is the Name of the Game

Everyone thinks change is based on what you're going to get, but change has a lot to do with what you're willing to get rid of—like a hot air balloon that goes up when you throw the sand out of it. A lot of people don't want to throw the sand out; they want to keep the sand and still go up.

Step 6: Were entirely ready to have God remove all these defects of character.

Step 7: Humbly asked Him to remove our shortcomings.

All the change that comes about through God working in our lives is by our consent and our permission. All the growth that happens, happens through our will and our consent. We have to make the decision. We have to become willing and ready, and we can see it building to the point of change.

Steps 6 and 7 are the pinnacle of the program. If we look back at the other Steps and see how they work, we can see that we took them to give us the ability to take Steps 6 and 7, where the changes can really begin. In Step 1 we saw the problem, in Step 2 we saw the solution, in Step 3 we made a decision, and in Step 4 we had to go to work to identify the things that blocked us. In Step 5 we re-examined those blocks, getting down to their exact nature, making sure they were fine-tuned.

Now we're ready to start changing. So Steps 1, 2, 3, 4, and 5 have put us into position for Steps 6 and 7—the changing process.

Sometimes getting self-awareness is painful. We've heard it said that the truth will make you free, but at first it will most likely make you miserable!

Step 6 is about becoming willing to let go. After all, we have worked for *years* with the things in our lives that cause us problems. We have made them a part of our lives. We have worked at our character defects and built them into our personalities! Through the power of Step 4, we have seen how damaging these character defects are. After discussing them further with someone else, we should now be willing to let go of them. But even if we are not willing to let go of them, the Step covers that, too—because we will pray for the willingness until it comes. (Prayer is useful throughout these Steps!)

But we aren't ready to let go of some of these character defects (or shortcomings, or whatever we choose to call them). Step 6 is getting the willingness to let go of them. Once we are willing, we ask God to remove them in Step 7. Steps 6 and 7 are companion Steps. They are not Steps we take one after another like the others. They're Steps we take *beside each other.* That is, we may see our defects gradually, over time, and we will use Steps 6 and 7 as we see them: we will become *willing to let go* of them and *ask God to remove them.*

There has been a lot of discussion about these Steps, but they are simple, basic tools of change. They are based on one of the oldest laws of human nature: whatever you practice, you become good at. Whether it's baseball, piano, or typing, you learn that skill because you work at it. You can't go to typing class, learn the *theory* of typing, and be a good typist. Once you take the ideas the instructor gives you and put them in your mind, then you have to *practice* those ideas to own them. After that, you own the ability to type. You can go out and sell it daily on the job because you own the skill—you own it through practice.

This is certainly the way we own our defects of character. We have accumulated them through years and years of practice. We have drilled them into our personalities. Our personalities are nothing but a pattern of mental habits we have accumulated and practiced and *made into* a pattern. Each one of us has molded an individual personality this way. Each one of us is a unique personality—in fact, our personalities are just as unique as our fingerprints. All of us have particular mental habits we have practiced.

Now that we have examined these things in Step 4, now that we have examined this set of patterns that we have, we see that some are unproductive. We should be willing to change them because they are not bringing any returns to our lives. In fact, they are bringing trouble.

We're actually going to use the same process in changing that we've used in developing this personality. That is, we'll have to *practice something different.* Now that we have examined these unproductive things in Steps 4 and 5, they should be objectionable to us. That's the key word: they should be *objectionable* to us. We should now see they are of no value to us. If we didn't do Steps 4 and 5, these things will not have become objectionable to us, and we will see no reason to change.

It's the power of these Steps that makes our defects, our unproductive attitudes, objectionable. Once we see them as objectionable, we will become ready to let go of them, and that's Step 6. Step 7 then comes into play: if we want to *change,* we will begin to *practice something different* to take the place of our defects and unproductive attitudes. We will change our personalities by the use of that principle, the principle of change.

If you want to change, you can't give in to the same old ideas produced by the same old thought patterns in the same old mind of the same old personality—our selfish, dishonest, self-seeking character. Remember, that character is there because we have practiced at it. No one can brainwash us. No one can wipe out or remove those ideas from our minds, because they are imbedded there.

But *we* can remove any objectionable idea from our minds by overriding it with better ideas. This is what we're going to try to do. Then when an old idea comes up, we can recognize it right away. When we see ourselves in an old familiar thought pattern, we say to ourselves: "This is not productive. I don't want to think like this. I know the outcome of this from before. I saw it in the inventory process and when I talked it over with someone else. There's no value in the same old outcome. I'm getting out of this."

That's *very hard to do* in the beginning. But if we don't lend our thoughts to those old unproductive ideas, they'll die in our minds. The Big Book assures us, "The old ideas will be cast aside and a new set of motives will begin to dominate the mind." (p. 27) As the old ideas die, then we can replace them with new ideas.

Step 6 is based on this truth: *if you want to change, you don't do what you want to do.* If you don't do what you want to do, you can slay that old idea with inaction.

In the New Testament the apostle Paul says that successful living means daily dying. (I Corinthians 15:31) Many people assume this means physical death, but I believe it means dying in certain areas of our ideas, so that we can live somewhere else. He said only *we* can slay ourselves. Successful living is daily dying. Only we can do that. We have to die in some small way so we can live in a better way.

The real problem is that most people cling to what they are, even though they don't like it. It's painful, but at least they're familiar with it! They're not ready to give up on that for something better.

I like to ask people, "How do you get a new car? What's the very first thing you do to get a new car?" Most people will say you start by looking in the newspaper or by going to the dealership, those kinds of things. That's not right. The *first* thing you have to do is *give up on the old car.* As long as you think "I can put new tires on" or whatever, you'll still have the old one. Somewhere along the line you say, "I'm through with this." *Then* you're on the road to a new car. This is what we have to do here in Steps 6 and 7: we have to give up in certain areas.

As we stop doing the things we want to do, we force ourselves to do the things we don't want to do. As we force ourselves to do these things, we get the benefits of these new thought patterns. They bring us different returns. We've learned that our lives are like a business: we have a certain stock-in-trade, and our lives are based on what we have on hand to trade in. If we are trading with better ideas, they're going to bring better returns into our business of living. As they bring in better returns, then we'll buy into these ideas even more and make them part of our personalities. We'll look at the new ideas and say, "These are valuable. I *like* these."

Over a very short period of time, we'll find ourselves noticing these new ideas becoming a part of our personalities. The old attitudes we used to act out will become less and less. New traits, backed by our new thoughts, will replace them. With different ideas, we have a different stock-in-trade, and we'll be getting different things back, so we'll be having a different life! Because, as we've said earlier, our lives are based on the ideas we produce in our minds!

Once you make yourself do those things that aren't easy or attractive to you, you will begin to see the rewards. But you can't receive rewards *unless you do it.* We can have all kinds of grand, philosophical ideas, but if we don't make them a part of our personalities and live them, they are of no value. Many people have great ideas, but those ideas are not really a part of their lives.

For instance, we can decide we don't want to gossip anymore. We all get into gossiping because others are into it. It's very hard to avoid. If somebody gossips, you can't just say, "Well, I don't gossip." You're afraid that if you did, nobody would talk to you. So you buy into it and listen. But I realize each time I'm involved in any gossip that what it is, is selfishness. By participating, I'm saying I'm better than this person being talked about. I am actually building my ego on somebody else's downfall.

We have taken the first five Steps. At this point, many people make the mistake of turning it over to God and expecting God to apply Steps 6 and 7 to their lives. But these are *our* Steps—God doesn't need to take Steps 6 and 7. We do.

One of the greatest mistakes people make with Steps 6 and 7 is thinking that it's some easy, automatic process. We turn it over to God and say, "Fix me up, give me the $29.95 special." It's not going to happen. Remember, we've been given self-will. Although we can't do it by ourselves, and we have to ask for the strength to do it, *only we can refashion our personalities.* If God controlled the personality, it would have never gotten in the shape we let it get in!

We can fashion this new personality based on what we've learned, the insights we've gained, in Steps 4 and 5. There are certain things we've seen that have become objectionable to us, so we begin to work against those things. We work against them and replace them, and the new things will then become our new character. We can use the new ideas and thought patterns, and get better returns. We can buy into them and let them become part of our lives. And we can also change that later, if need be.

We can go anywhere we want to go, most of the time, based on *what we want to give up.* Everyone thinks change is based on what you're going to get—but change has a lot to do with *what you're willing to get rid of.* It's like a hot air balloon that goes up when you throw the sand out of it. A lot of people don't want to throw the sand out; they want to keep the sand and *still* go up.

Remember, we are discovering the principles of living. They're universal and unchanging. Life is based on the principles. All the great religions teach the principles. There's a great similarity regardless of where we see them, in one group or the other. There's a great *oneness* in the principles of living. Behind everything is a principle: everything on the face of this earth, everything we make, everything we manufacture, has a set of principles behind it. *We* are created with a set of principles, too. There's a way to live; you can find it in many great books, all the great religions, any Twelve-Step program.

We look at the Twelve Steps as just simple principles, without a lot of instructions. And people show you how to use those principles. I think religion took the same principles, put a lot of instructions with them, added a lot of comment to them over a thousand years—to where now people can hardly find the principles in their programs. Often religious groups have gotten involved in other things and gotten away from the basic principles of how to live.

So the whole process from now on is change. We must be open, we must be willing, we must see the power of change. We must realize our inability to change anyone else. We can see all the frustrations this has brought into our lives. We have learned that the key to changing a situation from now on is to change ourselves, change our reactions, and not even try to change anybody else.

The best way to change things "out there" is to change ourselves. We change our *reactions,* and we are free. And ironically, by doing so, we may produce some changes out there.

When we were drinking or using drugs or pursuing any

other compulsion, we were trying to fill our emptiness up with the wrong things. Alcohol, drugs, food, control of other people—all of these are expressions of people who don't have the principles for living. These compulsions are just symptoms of the problem, and the Steps don't deal with symptoms. The Steps are not talking about dealing with alcohol, drugs, food, codependency. *The Steps teach us how to live.* If we're learning how to live and practicing the principles, then the problem won't be there—because it's just a symptom.

Whatever our compulsion or addiction is, it is only a symptom of an underlying illness. (There will never be enough of this thing we think we want when we're living lives based on self—never enough of what we think will satisfy us!) But if we use the program, we can get over our compulsion. It's a simple process. Not only do we get over it, but we find out the result of getting over it is that we get some living skills we'd never have gotten if we hadn't had the problem! So, actually, we come out of the situation a lot better than we went into it: we gain the tools to live by.

I always like to use the illustration of how to lose weight when we talk about the principle of change. If you want to change the body, you use the same principle as you use to change the mind. The body is the result of the food we put into it. (That's what our minds are—the result of the thoughts that we have put into them, from the very first one we had until today.)

If we want to change the body, we have to change the food we put into it. If you want to lose some weight, you have to stop eating the food you really like—maybe it's candy or fast foods, milk shakes and french fries and all that stuff. Those things are objectionable, and why are they objectionable? You looked in the mirror and saw yourself, you saw how you looked, and you saw the results of eating those foods. (When we looked in the "mirror" with Steps 4 and 5, we saw our personalities.)

Now those foods have become objectionable. If you want to change, then you have to not eat those foods. You have to deny yourself. When you don't eat those foods, you have to turn around and make yourself eat others that you probably don't like, some low-calorie foods, most likely salads, vegetables. You really don't like that stuff. What you really like is the other stuff, but you don't like what it's doing to you. As you work against your self, as you stop eating what you want to eat and start eating what you don't want to eat, you're going to see some changes in your body.

As your body begins to change and you start losing weight, you think better about yourself. Your self-esteem goes up, you can do things you couldn't do before, you have different relationships—your life is really beginning to change as a result of this. Then it's very interesting: people tell me that food they didn't like—the low-calorie stuff—they begin to like. They don't even want the things they used to anymore. Those new foods have become a part of their way of life.

The same thing happens in the human personality. We get rid of the old things and start practicing the new. With these new things—more love, tolerance, patience—we begin to have more people in our lives and fewer and fewer problems with people. As we receive more courage, we can do things we couldn't do before. Our self-esteem grows. We feel better about ourselves. As we practice the Steps, we see powerful changes taking place in our lives.

I look at the battles that go on in life, and I look at the resentments and fears, guilt and remorse, and how these things block us from God and shackle us to the self. Then I look at love, tolerance, patience, courage, and wisdom. These qualities have come from God, and they are always within us. In our outer and inner conflicts, we can see the powers of self combatting the powers of God. We look at those things—the powers of God we have within us—and recognize that they are powerful tools. We have not been using them because we were traveling on resentments, we were traveling on fears, we were traveling on guilt and remorse. Yet all people have these powers from God, powers for good, in their personalities. God put these in each person. These powers, these awesome forces are right within us. We haven't been using them because we have been blocked from them by clinging to our selfish, dishonest, self-seeking, fearful, inconsiderate characters. As we begin to let go of these traits, we

PERSONALITY CHART

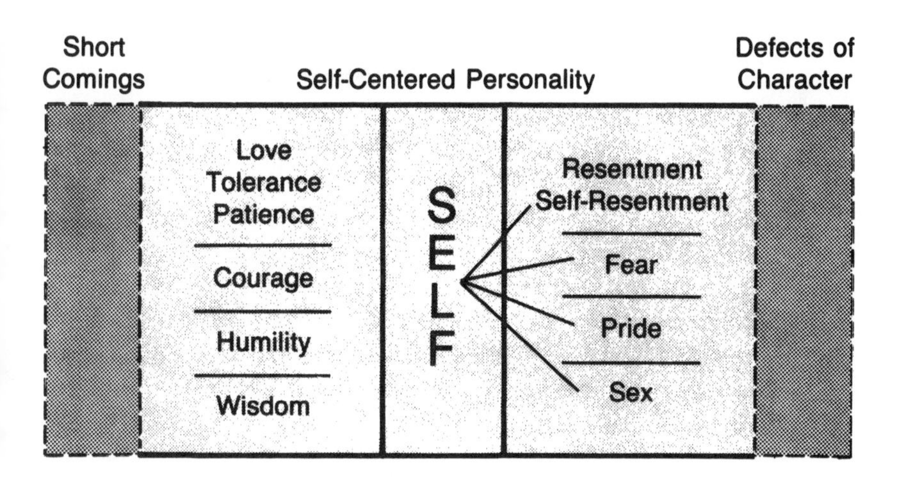

Balanced Personality

Love
Tolerance
Patience

Courage

Humility

Wisdom

GOD

Resentment
Self-Resentment

Fear

Pride

Sex

Qualities of God

Qualities of Man

begin to see the real qualities of God within us.

Our shortcomings are removed based on what we want to let go of. If we let go of fear, courage is going to come into our lives. If we don't practice resentments, we're going to see love, tolerance, patience, understanding, and good will coming into our lives. We practice those things and see our relationships with people grow.

These changes will come about, and we'll see the awesome power that lies within these forces. We can accomplish things each day that we never could do before. The Big Book says we can go places and do things that we never could before. The Big Book says we have tapped an "inner resource" of strength. (pp. 569-570) This is power.

You know, here's what a shortcoming is: when you're *long on resentments,* then you're necessarily *short on love, tolerance, and patience.* It's like sliding a scale. You're supposed to have some resentments—they're what makes you competitive—but if that side of the scale goes too far, then it makes you shorter on the side of the scale with the *real* powers of life, powers like love, tolerance, and patience. If you have too much resentment, you can't express the real powers, and you have to express either one or the other. Some people don't really see love in themselves. It's there, but it seems non-existent because it hasn't been expressed in the personality.

Just what *is* love? Love is basically concern for another person's welfare or for our own welfare. All of us are designed to have the ability to be concerned about ourselves and about each other. God put it in every person. Without our ability to be concerned about each other, the human race could not exist. We couldn't have families, neighborhoods, states, or nations.

Love is a bond that is natural. Most of the time we hear it expressed differently, like in the context of a male-female relationship, but love is a feeling we *all* feel. It's what makes us bond together. When a person does not have this ability to bond with others, then he's not fitting into the family, he's not fitting into relationships, he's not fitting into the society in general.

Love is a powerful force for healing. I like what Martin Luther King said—that love is the most powerful force on the

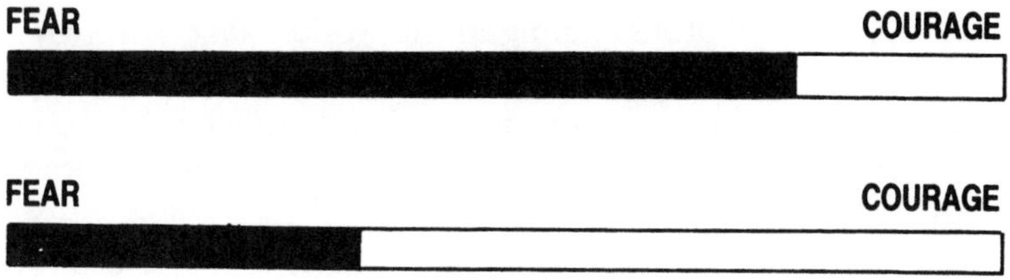

FEAR COURAGE

FEAR COURAGE

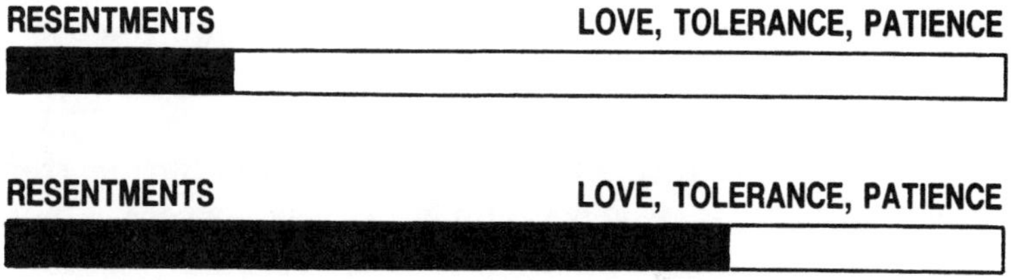

RESENTMENTS LOVE, TOLERANCE, PATIENCE

RESENTMENTS LOVE, TOLERANCE, PATIENCE

It's like sliding a scale. When you're long on fear, you're necessarily short on courage. When you're long on love, tolerance, and patience, you're short on resentments.

face of the earth. Gandhi said love is the only thing that could turn an enemy into a friend. It's an amazing thing—you take all the bombs and weapons we have, no matter how many we have, we'll never make friends with these weapons. But we could with love. And I see that happening in the world today. Through a series of circumstances that have happened in other countries, and also through our concern in helping them with their problems, we are seeing some downgrading of the ability to wage war!

Sometimes a person might say, "Well, I don't have these positive forces in me." They are so blocked, but down inside they do have them! As we begin to practice these new positive traits (love, patience, tolerance, for example), we begin to see the real value in them, and we find that we are developing true concern for other people.

And concern for ourselves as well. I ask a lot of people who come into the program, selfish, self-centered, and messed up with these character defects, "How concerned have you been for your own life for the last couple of years?" We need to learn the wisdom of "Love your neighbor as yourself."(Matthew 22:39) If you're not concerned about your own life, you can't be concerned about your neighbor simply because concern is not there.

To go out and do things for other people without this self-love is a token. It's hollow—you're trying to do something to cover up the hollowness inside of you. That's using other people. Or it's bargaining with God, trying to earn His love. We can't earn God's love, because it's free. Deep, true concern for others will come after we have realized our own value in God's eyes. Then it will grow with time, over the years.

Love is a two-way street: it has to be given and received. A lot of people don't have that ability because they can't receive. They can't let another person help them. If we can't receive, then we can't truly give. This ultimately makes for conflict, and we respond with resentments.

We really need to consider the power of giving up. We can ask ourselves in a certain situation, "What is it that I have to give up?" We're always looking at what we're going to get, but we should look for what we're going to give up and be able to spot that right away. It's usually simple—it's usually one of the character defects we've talked about.

> **How this "spirituality of subtraction" works was stated beautifully by Meister Eckhart, a 14th century mystic:**
>
> **"It is said that nature abhors a vacuum; I tell you God abhors a vacuum and cannot abide a vacuum anywhere on earth. So, empty yourself of self and you automatically fill with God."**

Here's how it works—when you get rid of a character defect, you have overcome a shortcoming! It's practically automatic. By nature's law, there can't be a void. There is no void in the universe. Something rushes in to fill a void. So if you're willing to let go of a defect, the void it leaves is going to be filled by its opposite. Fear is going to be replaced with courage; resentments with love, tolerance, patience, understanding, good will towards others. When you let go of one, it's not going to leave a hole, a blank spot. This positive thing will be there to take its place. Nobody had to teach me love, tolerance and patience. I had never used them, but they were there.

This process is sometimes frightening. I used to say to myself, "I'm some kind of freak because I don't have that positive quality. I never have done that—maybe I was created without the ability, and I'll have to learn it." I didn't have to learn it, though. When I got rid of other things, it was already there!

I have a pretty rocking chair down in my office. When I first bought that building, someone had run off and left it behind. There wasn't anything there of any value, but there was this old rocking chair. It was just a horrible-looking mess, painted black, with one of the rungs broken out of the back of it. I decided I'd keep it, thinking maybe one of these days I might put it together.

Quite a few years went by and it just sat in the attic. Several times some of the guys tempted me to throw it away; in fact, I'd find it around by the dumpster and I'd bring it back, saying I was going to look at it one of these days.

So I finally got this old rocking chair out of the attic and into the light downstairs so I could really see it. And I began to look at it, and I saw that it was a really fine chair. I got some paint stripper, and I began to strip it. I stripped all the paint away and found that it was solid oak. I took the old raggedy bottom that had been covered over many, many times with different cloth and with tacks, and I tore it off and threw it all away. There was one broken rung and I made an identical one by bending one and putting it in there. I sanded and sanded and refinished this chair.

Finally, I took it to the upholstery shop. I asked the man there how much it would cost to put a nice white velvet bottom in it. He looked at it and said, "I'll be glad to put it in there, but before I fix it, I'll offer you $350 for that chair." That beautiful, valuable chair was always there. It was there all the time! It was simply covered up. That chair has always been beautiful since the day the guy made it. And that's the way I am—and you are—with God's life inside us. God made us this way—beautiful and valuable.

Like the rocking chair, over a period of years, I covered myself up with all sorts of things and made a big mess. The Steps of this program have enabled me to uncover, discover, and discard. It's a program of getting rid of things to get down to what we want. It's not a program of getting anything. It's a program of getting rid of things: *uncovering, discovering, and discarding.*

I believe that deep down inside everyone is the fundamental idea of God. We might have covered it up, but it's there. Regardless of what we see in the most horrible individual, down underneath he still has the qualities of God to live by. He may not be using them, and we may punish him for his actions, but he is created with these things—these God-qualities. Each and every one of us is.

We don't have to go out and look for them. All we have to do is convince ourselves that they are already there. Our personalities are just like gold. You have to really dig to get it. That's why it has value. If gold could be found all over the streets, everybody could get all they wanted. That might be great, but then gold wouldn't have any value. There would be too much of it, and it would be too easily found.

It's the same way with life. It may take a lot of digging, scraping, a lot of mining; that's what we're doing in Steps 6 and 7. But remember, we're mining for gold! For our innermost selves!

This is what's fascinating about Steps 6 and 7—this looking into ourselves and going after our own gold, our God-qualities. Of course, this gold-mining we're talking about is a lifetime task. But whatever our immediate problem is—our compulsion or addiction—we can be surprised at the progress we make in a few months. We may have a change sufficient to recover in 100 days. According to the Big Book, we can change the personality by use of the principles in Steps 6 and 7, by working against some traits, in 100 days. Then we can go on and on with the process for the rest of our lives. The first, early changes get us on the road, put us in sight of our goal: to grow spiritually.

Like with patience, for example. You can't really work on patience. But if you use patience, you see the power of it, the power of the ability to wait. Sitting and waiting for a street light to change, even little things such as this can make us impatient. Well, you've got to sit there anyway, so you might as well enjoy it. I've had a lot of people tell me that in reading directions for glue, the directions may say "wait five minutes," and in two minutes they're putting their finger in there because they don't have the little bit of patience to wait.

Patience is accepting God's timing in life. There's timing in everything. Just like with glue, so it is with growth. There is a time process involved in everything. Patience is the ability to allow the time for things to work. The individual has to fit into the timing, and patience is the ability to fit into the timing of life. If we don't fit into the timing of life, then we experience frustrations, irritations—simply because we are not letting life happen. *We are trying to make life happen on our time, which it never will.* So patience—the ability to wait, to fit the timing of life—is a powerful tool.

We may get up every day and have plans. It's okay to have plans. Most of us get up and think about our day at work, for example, about what we're going to do that day. You're mentally fitting all this in, trying to fit in twice as much as you can get done. But you head for work, and the Fire Dept. has the street blocked off. So what we're talking about here is that plans are great, but *our plans have to be open to change.* We have to be able to adjust throughout the day *and let things happen.* Some days I have certain plans and everything falls into place just fine—it's unbelievable—and on that kind of day I figure I'll get everything

How to React and Not React

Sometimes others say to us, "I wouldn't take that!" or "Why don't you do this?" We hear this kind of thing all the time. In fact, it's becoming some kind of vogue thing to be sick, to express. We hear, "Tell him off; don't take that; stand up for yourself." Those things are not really healthy ways to live. Sometimes it's better to let a sick person be sick, and accept his sickness—better to think to ourselves "he's a little messed up today ... he's in a bad mood." If we accept, we can use a little love, tolerance, and patience. We can find the power of these things. Sometimes a person comes up to you full of resentments and says, "I want to talk to you ... and I don't like this ... " You can simply say, "Well, you're right ... you know, I'm sorry." You have changed the game. I have the ability to change the game. When you come up to me with an attitude, I don't have to express your attitude. I have the right to decide what attitude I'm going to express, to react to you with. It's a big thing, you know. It's like playing cards. If you're going to play cards with me, you can play with my deck, not yours. If you come up to me, with resentments and I buy into your resentments, then I'm playing with your deck.

done that I can. Other days it just won't happen.

Here's how Steps 6 and 7 most often happen: We go through a period of time when we ask, "What's wrong with me?" We get so much new self-awareness, awareness of our character defects. As we see things that we want to change and work against these things, we (and others) will see the personality change begin to take place. We will have different responses to situations. This is the key to our growth: we realize we can't change the situation or other people, but we can change our response to it!

I remember when I was very new and going through all

When you think you have to prove you're right and he's wrong, that's ego. Let him be right or wrong. If he doesn't want you to be right, he's not going to see it anyway. It's the way he feels about something, the way he's looking at it. He's probably always going to see it that way.

I like what Harry Truman said. They asked him if he ever made a mistake and he said, "You're damn right, and it didn't take me all day to do it, either." I see a lot of fine people who shock me by always defending. There's something shallow about that. Once we begin to spot that weakness, we can take care of it and become stronger.

Sometimes people point out things to us; maybe they're doing it with good intentions, not so much to put us down, but out of true concern. The more we can accept this, as our personality develops more and more, people will be helping us in that way. But if we're real defensive, nobody's going to tell us anything. A lot of times I've grown because somebody close would tell me, when I'm wrong. I think that's growth. When you're always right and you know everything, nobody's going to tell you anything.

these changes, a situation came up at work and I got in an unpleasant discussion with the manager. I felt real bad about it. I saw that I was wrong. It was the first time in years I could remember seeing that. That was some growth taking place in me. I went to this guy—I'll never forget, he was closing up for the night and he was counting money, he was preoccupied—and I told him I wanted to talk to him. I said I wanted to make amends to him for what I said when this thing came up.

"What was that?" he said. I went on to explain to him, and he said, "It was nothing—it just came under the heat of us being busy." I remember how good I felt when I went home that night. It was like experiencing something brand new. I could see the value of it.

Remember, we never know the value of something until we put it into our stock-in-trade. Like a businessman, if he's selling shoddy goods, he'll never know how many customers he would have if he put something really good in. And he may never know what a truly successful business is.

All of us are different people; no two of us have the same desires or motivations. Thank God we don't. We will always be individual personalities. No two of us start from the same place. No two of us are going to end up in the same place. I think along the road each one of us will fashion a much better life with the tools of change the program gives us. Change is the name of the game. As God reveals things to us, we can make changes. And we can continue to grow and grow forever. We can give up and grow, give up and grow, and this is unending.

Making Amends

What we are doing here is getting rid of what Bill called "our grosser handicaps." These are things that dominate our minds. Remember, we have committed ourselves to the whole process. We can't just stop here and say, "I'm going to leave this part off." It's like making a cake: if your recipe has twelve steps in it, and you just do seven and stop, you don't have a cake!

Step 8: Made a list of all persons we had harmed and became willing to make amends to them all.

Step 9: Made direct amends to such people wherever possible, except when to do so would injure them or others.

People are usually reluctant and sometimes fearful about Steps 8 and 9 and the process they require. These are the last actions that we have to take before the promises start to be fulfilled. This encourages us to take these Steps even though they may cause us some fear.

One of the main things we are doing with these Steps is carrying out the decision we made in Step 3: removing the things that block us from God. It's easy to see how this works, because one of the biggest things that has blocked us from God is our guilt and remorse over the harms we have done to others in the past. Our resentments have turned our lives over to others. The same is true of fear: when we fear something, the fear dominates us. And if we have guilt and remorse over something we have done in the past, then we are letting this control our minds in the present.

There is no way God can control our minds when our minds are being dominated by something that occurred in the past. Our only way to get rid of these blocks is to clear them up. This is the process of Steps 8 and 9. These Steps are the last hurdle of getting rid of the guilt and remorse we have over things we've done in the past. This simple process is outlined in a way that anyone can follow.

First, we are told to make a list of all the people we have harmed. If we look at one part of the process at a time and complete it in phases, we can see how easy it is to make a list of the people we have harmed. The Big Book says we should have made it when we took the inventory. If we have done the inventory as the Big Book instructed us, we made out a list of resentments and analyzed it. After we analyzed the list, we found out that we had done something to some of those people listed in the first column, and that our resentment was based on their retaliation for something for which we owe them amends.

People

INSTRUCTIONS FOR COMPLETION

List the people you have harmed in any way.
A. Listing from top to bottom.
B. List what you did.
C. What part of self caused you the harm? (Column 3)
D. What character defect was involved? (Column 4)

	COLUMN 1	COLUMN 2
	Whom did I hurt?	What did I do?
1		
2		
3		
4		
5		
6		
7		

Have Harmed

"SELF" COLUMN 3									COLUMN 4			
Affects My... (Which part of self caused the harm?)									What is the exact nature of my wrongs, faults, mistakes, defects, shortcomings:			
Social Instinct		Security Instinct		Sex Instinct		Ambitions						
Self-Esteem	Personal Relationships	Material	Emotional	Acceptable Sex Relations	Hidden Sex Relations	Social	Security	Sexual	Selfish	Dishonest	Self-Seeking Frightened	Incnsiderate

We may have done something to them based on self and covered up our guilt by being resentful. So we have cleared up the resentment part of that as we analyzed it.

Now we want to go back and clear up the guilt and remorse associated with people on our lists. We find some people on our fear list. These were people—and maybe institutions—to whom we had done something in the past because we feared them. Quite naturally, some names are on our sex conduct list. So we have three groups of people whom we have harmed already.

After we have completed that, we should put down the names of any other people we have harmed in any way. First we list the names, then what we did, then what part of self caused us to do it. Then we list which character defect was involved in that particular harm. The advantage is this: if you can list and analyze people you have harmed, in the same way you did on your lists of resentments, fears, and sex conduct, you'll see which part of self was involved in each harm, and you'll see which part of your character was associated with that harm.

The more in-depth knowledge we have of ourselves and our relationships to people, the more we see how we were involved, the more we will be willing to make amends to those people. If we don't see those things, usually we make hollow amends, or don't get into it enough to benefit from it. If we can see the detail of harms we have done, we're more likely to make sincere and beneficial amends and clear those things up. This is why we were asked to make that list while we were making our inventory. It's easier to make the list while you are making the detailed inventory in Step 4 than it is to wait until you get to Step 8. If you wait, you won't have all the behind-the-scenes information you need to understand the whole thing.

So the first part of Step 8 should be completed when you have done the inventory. The second part of this Step says "...became willing to make amends to them all." We must become willing to do this, and if we are not willing, *we pray for the willingness until it comes.* We say that each Step has its prayer, and this is the Step 8 prayer. Willingness—here, as in the rest of the Steps—is the key. When we become willing, we often experience relief even before we get a chance to make the amends.

The willingness is what frees us.

Even if making the amends we need to make would injure someone and we can't actually make them, when we become *willing* we are freed from the guilt and remorse that have kept us back. We have to be sure and get this point across: we are doing this for ourselves, not for the benefit it may bring to the person we are making amends to. We are trying to remove the things that block us from God. We take these Steps for our own recovery. We are not considering what they may do for others; this is not our purpose.

Once we get the list and become willing to make amends, then we can go into Step 9, which continues the process, and make "direct amends." The Big Book has dealt very extensively with Step 9 because there are a lot of things that can come up. In the chapter entitled "Into Action," a number of specific situations are given as examples (beginning on p. 76 and continuing for several pages). This chapter is worth close study.

Step 9 tells us to make "direct amends." What are direct amends? Direct amends are face-to-face amends to the person you have harmed. Later on in the Big Book it says you can write a letter to a person you've harmed, but the first example is of going to see a man in his office. We are told not to discuss his problems, but to discuss the reason we've come. If we are thrown out of the office, we are not to consider our mission a failure, because his response is not the primary thing. The most important thing is that we have been *willing to* and we have *attempted to* make the amends. You will get more relief from the guilt and remorse in a face-to-face making of amends than you will from writing a letter, or even from making amends on the telephone.

I heard of a guy who asked his sponsor if he could make his amends by mail. His sponsor is supposed to have said, "Sure you can—if you harmed them by mail."

Step 9 tells us to make "direct amends" and then tells us "wherever possible." A lot of people think it says "whenever possible," but it doesn't. It says *"wherever* possible." I think this is the spirituality in this Step. It's God working in this phase of our lives. We don't have to worry about all these amends that we need to make coming down at one time. God knows when we are ready, and he will give us—or help us get—the opportunity to make the amends we are willing to make in good time. Again, the key thing is to be willing. If we are willing, we can wait till God's time.

I think a mistake many people make is in thinking Step 9 is like Step 1 and must be made one hundred percent at one time. But if we try to make a whole list of the people we have harmed and try to run out the door and make our amends that same day, we are usually going to make a lot of problems for ourselves and for other people, too. Of course, we want to get the relief that comes from getting these things cleared up, but the key thing is to be willing.

There are a lot of people we can go to right away: our parents, for instance. They are usually fairly easy to make amends to because they love us and will often go that extra mile for us. You will most likely be surprised how a few months of recovery in a life will bring about a different understanding in the people we have hurt. They may know we have been making excuses for ourselves all our lives, but after they see us in recovery for a little while, they are probably going to be more receptive. The timing will be better. And remember, if we are willing, God will take care of the "wherever possible."

To make a beginning on the amends, we can divide them up into four lists. One list is of people we are ready to make amends to now. These are people like parents, spouses, others we are comfortable making amends to now. We should make a heading, and call this first group NOW.

Make a chart with these headings:

NOW	**LATER**	**I MAY AND I MAY NOT**	**NEVER**

Then we can have another list we call LATER. The third list we call I MAY AND I MAY NOT. The fourth list we call NEVER. (These are people you don't think you can ever make amends to because of what they did to you or because your guilt and remorse are too heavy.)

First, we do the easiest ones in the first column. When we get the relief and satisfaction from doing them, we will probably go to work on the LATERS, then on some MAYBES, and then probably we'll even get to some of those in the fourth column, the NEVERS.

What this system does is allow you a place to start. A lot of people having difficulty in their lives have such a negative viewpoint that they'll take the two or three names they can't face, and let these stop them from even beginning the process. But instead, we turn it around, start on the easiest ones, and leave those we feel we can't face until last. Remember, we never get the result of a Step until we take it, but once we start making amends to those people on our NOW list and we receive what we are going to get from doing it, it will encourage us to go on. The key thing is the starting point, and sometimes those great big, difficult ones will block us from starting, and we'll lie around and never work on them.

So we have to let God take care of the timing. Some people make the mistake of running out and trying to do it all right away, and some people won't do any of it. I think there are some amends we can make right away. The idea is to sort those out, and make a beginning.

The Big Book goes on to tell us we can't make amends that are going to hurt other people. There is an example of a man who needed to make amends which would implicate other people, so he went to them and got their permission. They allowed him to make the amends. (p. 80) But there are some amends we can't make because of the potential harm to other people. In these cases, we will just have to live with it. But I don't think these will be very painful, because the willingness we feel will give us a lot of relief. And later on, the situation might change so that it will no longer harm someone else, and then it goes on our list of amends to be made.

These Steps are where we need to be careful, and a new person really needs a sponsor to help make the right judgment calls. We are going to be working on some of these things for the rest of our lives. Most people have some things in their pasts they will have to always live with. (These burdens can even be beneficial, because they can make us treasure the new relationships we make as we recover and bring people back into our lives.) So while we have to become one hundred percent willing to make amends for all the harms we have caused, we must realize that we may work for a lifetime trying to make all the amends.

There are several reasons that may keep amends from falling into the "wherever possible" category: some people are dead, we don't know where some people are, some people we owe money and we simply don't have the money. (Regarding money, Bill tells us to make arrangements to pay when we can't pay immediately.) There were some amends I was never able to make, and I had some guilt and remorse about them. Then I began to find I could talk about them to people I was working with, and I realized that I was free. These were things I once couldn't talk about, and then I realized I was talking freely with people about them without guilt or pain.

Step 8:
1. Make a list of all people we have harmed.
2. Become willing to make amends to the people on the list.

Step 9:
3. Make direct amends to all the people on list, with the exception of those people in items #4 and #5 below.
4. Remove those from the list to whom it is impossible to make amends.
5. Remove those from the list for whom amends would produce injury.

You know, we are all living in God's world, and we all have God within us. Things even out. Sometimes I think a lot of our guilt and remorse is just our egos, anyway. One of the most important things we can learn from working these Steps is the value of other people if we want to have successful lives.

AN OLD SAYING:

MANY PEOPLE LOVE THINGS AND USE PEOPLE. WE MUST LEARN TO USE THINGS AND LOVE PEOPLE.

Most selfish, self-centered people have seen other people as something to be used instead of as valuable assets to a good life. They have run people off; they don't really see the purpose of having other people in their lives. Most self-centered people keep on being selfish and self-centered until they become successful at it, and they end up alone! That's what they have worked at all their lives: getting other people out of their lives.

But human beings were made to rely on God and each other. People who try to rely on self cut themselves off from God and other people and make their lives hard. So we can see that Steps 8 and 9 are ways we can put the things back in our lives that we need—a relationship with God and nurturing relationships with other people. We will not be using people as we did in the past, but we will see how we need people. The more successfully a person is living, the more people he has in his life, while the selfish, self-centered person will drive people out of his life.

While we need to learn to have nurturing, healthy relationships with other people, we also need to emphasize that we are not making these amends for the purpose of getting people to like us. Sometimes we may get thrown out of someone's office when we try to make amends, but that's the other person's problem, not ours. If we have made our amends and done our part, then it doesn't make any difference. If they still have a problem, we can let them have it.

A lot of times we don't realize that some of the attitudes people have toward us have been based on what we have been doing, and that's why they may have struck us or hurt us. It was our actions that gave them that attitude.

A lot of times we feel people are plotting against us, but we really have to be self-centered to think that—because *most people are actually not thinking about us at all.* Most people have better things to think about. There's a joke about a guy at a football game who thought that every time the players huddled out on the field, they were talking about him! I think it's natural for us to be concerned with what other people think, because that helps us monitor our behavior. We have to have some concerns for what others think. But, you know, it's like water: we have to have water to bathe in and to drink, but we don't want twenty feet of it standing in the street. That's a disaster.

A lot of times we don't have a very good sense of self-worth and *we try to use people to verify ourselves.* Once we have done Step 4 and begun to know ourselves and like ourselves, then our relationships are built on something firm. Then relationships can be healthy for us and for other people.

These Steps are a process, and we have already worked the first seven Steps. What will happen if we don't go ahead and take Steps 8 and 9? We won't get over the guilt and remorse, and they will come back in our minds and produce fear. We are going to have to hide from these people; we are going to have to avoid people that we owe money to. That fear is going to produce some self-pity and resentment. This will block us off from the decision we made in Step 3 and from the "sunlight of the Spirit," as Bill W. put it. (Big Book, p. 66) The chances are good that we are going to drink again or go back to our compulsive behavior. What may happen if we do Steps 1-7 perfectly and then don't do Steps 8 and 9 is that we may lose everything we have accomplished.

What we are doing here is getting rid of what Bill called "our grosser handicaps." These are things that dominate our minds. Remember, we have committed ourselves to the whole process. We can't just stop here and say, "I'm going to leave this part off." It's like making a cake: if your recipe has twelve steps in it, and you just do seven and stop, you don't have a cake! Your ingredients and the effort you've already put into the first seven steps will be wasted.

These are our grosser handicaps: resentment, fear, and guilt and remorse about the past. If we don't do Steps 8 and 9, these things continue to dominate our minds and block us off from God. Most of the negative things which go on in our minds can be put under one of these headings—either resentment (or self-pity, which is also resentment), or some form of fear, or guilt and remorse for something we have done or haven't done.

The completion of Steps 8 and 9 is the culmination of the action Steps. Now we are ready to receive the "promises." These promises are really the things that we've been looking for all along:

> We are going to know a new freedom and a new happiness. We will not regret the past nor wish to shut the door on it. We will comprehend the word serenity and we will know peace. No matter how far down the scale we have gone, we will see how our experience can benefit others. That feeling of uselessness and self-pity will disappear. We will lose interest in selfish things and gain interest in our fellows. Self-seeking will slip away. Our whole attitude and outlook upon life will change. Fear of people and of economic insecurity will leave us. We will intuitively know how to handle situations that used to baffle us. We will suddenly realize that God is doing for us what we could not do for ourselves.
>
> Big Book, pp. 83-84

If we look at the promises, we will see that these are the things we were trying to get from our old destructive practices. We were trying to wrestle these things out of life with alcohol, drugs, food, relationships, gambling, or whatever escape we were using. Now that we have removed these things that blocked us from God, now that we have tapped this "unsuspected inner resource" (p. 569-570), we have found a Power more beneficial than the "power" we found in alcohol or drugs or other compulsions.

At one time, the power of these things seemed satisfactory to us; then they turned on us and became our destruction. We abandoned them in Step 1, and made a decision in Step 3 on a new Power we had begun to find in Step 2. With Step 9, we have completed the actions. We have found the inner resource of strength—and that Power has solved our worst problems.

Continuing to Grow

Love, courage, tolerance, patience—these are powerful things that we can use in our lives. Step 10 is there to nurture these things. They are unlimited, and as we practice them on a daily basis, we find they continue to grow.

Step 10: Continued to take personal inventory and when we were wrong promptly admitted it.

The key to understanding the tenth Step is the word *continued.* After we have finished working the first nine Steps, there is really nothing new, but instead there is a continuous working of what we have already done.

If we go back through the Steps, we see that the first personality change occurs after Step 4: "We have begun to learn tolerance, patience and good will toward all men, even our enemies." (Big Book, p.70) And then we get a lot of growth after Step 5 and a lot of growth again after Step 9. All the growth will come through the action Steps. We don't get any real growth out of identifying the problem in Step 1 or finding the solution in Step 2. Step 3 is just a decision, and we don't get any growth from making a decision. All the real growth comes from Steps 4-9.

If we examine Step 10, we see it is a continuous practicing of those Steps (4-9) on a daily basis. There is no way we could enter a program like this and remain the same. The Big Book tells us to continue to watch for selfishness, dishonesty, resentment and fear, and we discovered those things in the fourth Step. When we find them, we discuss them with another person, which is Step 5. We asked God to remove them, which is Steps 6 and 7, and if we have harmed anyone, we make amends, which is Step 9. *So really Step 10 is a continuous practicing of Steps 4-9 on a daily basis.*

As we practice these Steps over and over, we will learn more and more about ourselves. We will see more and more character defects, and as we discuss them with someone else in Step 5, we will learn more and more. (Big Book, p. 83) As we ask God to remove them, they will become less and less. As we make amends to other people, our relationships with other people will grow better.

When we finish Step 9 we get the Promises. For all intents and purposes we have recovered. We have put our lives in order.

The Big Book talks about the three dimensions of life: the spirit, the mind, and the body. The Big Book gives us a design of living. Most people don't understand that life does have a design. First, we have a spiritual life, and we can live it in harmony or disharmony. It's sad, but most people live with it in disharmony. Many people go and do what they want to do, and *then* listen to their inner direction—rather than listening to it, and then deciding what to do.

We all have a mind, whether we always act like it or not. This is the second dimension of our lives. We are realizing today that mental health is based on spiritual health. Our physical lives emanate from the mind. When we say "physical lives" here, we are not just thinking about our physical bodies, but about everything in the physical world—everything we can see, everything society sees as our lives. So life emanates from the inside out, from the spiritual to the mental to the physical. Every great thinker, every great religion says this.

Jesus said, "Thou shalt love the Lord thy God with all thy heart"—that's the center, the spirit—"with all thy mind"—that's our second division—"and thy neighbor as thyself." (Matthew 22:37-39) These are our Steps: Steps 1, 2, and 3 are the "the heart"; Steps 4, 5, 6, and 7 are the "mind"; and Steps 8 and 9 deal with our "neighbors," our relationships with others.

Our Steps work along the design of life. This is nothing new. This knowledge is as old as man himself. The power of it is that through the first nine Steps we have put our lives in order. Through these nine simple Steps! The miracle of the program of Alcoholics Anonymous is that it has boiled all the principles of living down into these Steps. These Steps correct anything that is wrong with our living, and the Promises come to us after those three dimensions of our lives are in order.

Steps 10, 11, and 12 come along next. They are different. The Big Book talks about a "fourth dimension" of existence which a lot of us don't really understand. Some of us have found a way of life that we never thought existed. Some of us know a little bit about heaven. (See Big Book, p. 25.) If we can grow spiritually and mentally and in right relationship with the physical world, we are going to expand into the "fourth dimension." As we grow, we will begin to occupy that fourth dimension the Big Book talks about.

In Step 3, we have made a decision to turn our lives over to the will of God, and that is about as perfectly as we can do that. God will take care of our growth; *all we have to do is remove the things that block us from God.* The only way to do that is through Steps 4, 5, 6, 7, 8 and 9. The spirit will then grow. If the spirit grows, the mind will grow, and when the mind grows, our relationships with other people and the rest of the physical world will grow, too. This growth is unending, and Step 10 is the beginning of this growth in our lives.

Step 10 is a way to enter the plan of continuous growth. We can't remain at a certain point. Everything is either growing or deteriorating. You might look at a stone building and think that it is not changing, but it is actually deteriorating. This is why we practice these Steps, these principles, on a daily, continuous basis.

A good, healthy Step 10 is always based on how well we have understood Steps 4, 5, 6, 7, 8 and 9. We find that some people cannot work Step 10 because they haven't done the other Steps effectively and thoroughly. Steps 4, 5, 6, 7, 8, and 9 are the tools that are built into Step 10, so if you can't do *them,* you can't work Step 10.

I think the inventory is probably the basis of our preparation. In the inventory we said that things emanate from the inside out, that it was really our character defects which caused the resentments. But we analyzed them from the outside in. We looked at the resentments first (the person we resented). Then we looked at what they had done, and then we traced that over to see which part of self was threatened. We traced *that* to find out the exact nature of our wrongs or character defects. Having done it that way, *when we come to Step 10, each day throughout the day, and throughout our lives, we use these tools when a resentment comes up.*

Most of our discomforts are caused by one of our grosser handicaps. (Remember, the Big Book says our grosser handicaps are resentments, fears, and guilt and remorse for something we have or have not done in the past.) Most of our uncomfortable feelings will fit under one of these categories. A lot of times we can call our uncomfortable feelings something else, but such feelings are usually based on our basic character defects.

WE NEED TO ASK OURSELVES:

AM I BEING SELFISH?
AM I BEING SELF-SEEKING?
AM I BEING DISHONEST?
AM I BEING INCONSIDERATE?
AM I BEING FEARFUL?

When we *feel* something, we try to find out what it is. We can say, "I've got a resentment." Now, we don't have to figure out who did something to us—that's going the wrong way. Instead, *we try to see which part of self has been threatened.* We don't pay attention to the first two columns; we go immediately to the third column. We ask, "What part of me has been threatened?" We know that *something* has been threatened, or we wouldn't have a feeling like this. Then we can say which character defect has come to the surface. You can spot it right away. It's one of these things: selfishness, dishonesty, lack of consideration, fear, or self-seeking. Most likely, one of these has come back into the personality. Once we identify it, we can deal with it. We might feel that we need to talk it over with another person, but not always.

The key thing here, as in any other illness, is early detection. Step 10 tells us *to detect these things early.* A lot of times they are like some of what we wrote down in Step 4, and identifying them is sometimes enough—they look stupid, and they just go away. When we catch ourselves back in those patterns again, we can often analyze them in our minds and deal with them, because we have learned to do it in Step 4.

We are promised in the Big Book "a new freedom." (p. 83) We have had to do a lot of work for this new freedom, and it can be protected. As soon as I feel a resentment and say, "It's so-and-so's fault," I realize I'm giving up my new freedom. I'm turning the reins of my life back over to someone else. The secret is that if it's my fault, I have a chance to be free. I always say, "I hope it's my fault."

It's so easy to go back to the old pattern of saying, "They did this or that to me!" But if we do, we will either go back to our old way of living, or at least we will be miserable. The key thing is to detect discomfort early, analyze it right away, and work your way right out of it.

It's a lot easier to do it this way than to do it the way most people do who are new and just learning the program. Many times they don't see the advantage of *immediately* doing this naming, analyzing, and letting go. They'll let these things pile up and pile up, until they have to go to someone in the program and get some help to get out from under the mess. Most people learn pretty fast after a little early help. After a while, you get skilled at spotting trouble right away.

After we take on this challenge for a while, it becomes exciting. The more we do Step 10, the more we learn about ourselves. It becomes a project. This is healthy. We've been running from ourselves for so long, and now we can take an interest in ourselves. It's not a negative kind of self-centeredness. Instead, we begin to see what we may contribute to life, what our talents may be, what our lives are all about. This kind of self-interest is healthy. We can now have goals and ways to meet our goals. We can have success and a purpose for living.

Since we are told to do it daily, people interpret the tenth Step as a Step that you do once a day. Many people think you're supposed to do it before bed at night, but we should work Step 10 *throughout the day.* A lot of people interpret this Step as meaning that just before we go to bed, we should look to see if we hurt anybody that day and ask for forgiveness and jump in bed. But most of us humans get into trouble in the daytime, not when we are in bed asleep.

I think this Step *does* mean that when we hurt anyone, we set it right, because that's related to Steps 8 and 9. "...When we were wrong, promptly admitted it" also means *we admit to ourselves when we are once again in a troublesome, uncomfortable behavior or way of thinking.* Of course, we know better now and we can try to get out of it in a hurry, but often we humans don't respond to emotional pain like we respond to physical pain.

Usually when we have physical pain, we know it indicates something is wrong, and we stop immediately to see what we can do to relieve it. With emotional pain, we sometimes just take it on and try to live with it instead of trying to find out what is causing it. But emotional pain, too, is a sign that something is wrong. With us, it is a sign that our character has gotten off its track. *Pain is a symptom* in both cases, physical and emotional. When we have emotional pain we should be aware that *something has gone wrong or is about to go wrong*—and we should nip it in the bud. We deal with it, instead of sweeping it under the rug and letting it get really bad. If we can do that effectively we will grow.

We are not encouraged to just talk about it—this is a positive program where we can deal with emotional pain and eliminate it. I think one of the mistakes many people are making today is this: not only individuals, but groups of people, get together and talk about their problems. They never seem to talk about what to *do* about them—they just discuss them over and over. They love to get with their friends and say, "I had a bad day. Tell me what yours was like." There is no growth in this way of doing. In fact, they just magnify their problems. I call this "group sickness." This is not what we are talking about.

We are talking about a positive program where we look at problems head-on, analyze them, get down to the causes and conditions, and use the tools we've learned to use to get rid of the problems. The more we use these tools, the more skilled we're going to become with them (that is, Steps 4, 5, 6, 7, 8, and 9). For example, once we have made amends a few times, we are going to find that we are able to just go and do it when we need to, without the dread that we had at first.

So Step 10 is not a new process. It's Steps 4, 5, 6, 7, 8, and 9 *done every day as a habit.* We are learning about tools–tools for living. People in the religions have these tools, but often they just tell people, "You ought to have a spiritual experience and live in harmony with God and your fellow man." They fail to give people a *program,* the tools that will enable them to have a spiritual experience and live in harmony.

Christianity has all the simplicity of these Steps. In fact, Christianity is what these Steps are based on, but the people who teach others about Christianity often fail to take the time to point the important things out to their people. I think this is caused by haste: people need direction, step-by-step direction on a personal basis, and this takes a lot of time. Lots of people keep hanging around, but they never learn it.

I think what's so *powerful* about the Twelve Steps is that they have been boiled down to such a simple process. I imagine Christianity was this simple at first.

So, Step 10 is not something we do before we go to bed at night. It is something we do all through the day. It is very easy—as soon as we feel something out of line, some discomfort—to pause, analyze it, find out what it was, and get rid of it. If we don't, the chances are it's going to build up and ruin our day. It's sort of like a drain stopping up. Sometimes a few little hair-like roots can grow through a pipe, seemingly not enough to do any harm, but when a little trash starts to pile up against those little roots, pretty soon you have a stopped-up drain. We can start off getting a little irritated with our car, then we get a little irritated with the children, and pretty soon we've wasted a whole day.

There is a prayer I like which says, "We are given a day; we are given the bread for the day." Bread means strength. We are given what we need for each day. If we use it as we are supposed to, we can deal with each day, one day at a time. We have the substance for each day, as the prayer says. We have the strength and courage and knowledge, and everything else we may need, to deal with things on a daily basis. What we have to do is work our program so that the negative things don't pile up. This is what Step 10 is for. It is our maintenance Step that keeps us open to the strength that is naturally ours.

After we work Step 10, we have a new list of promises in the Big Book (pp. 84-85) that people overlook sometimes. We're told we will now be restored to sanity, and we will have a new attitude toward alcohol (or whatever addiction or compulsion we may have had, of course). We're told we were insane in one area, but now we see it in a different light, "and we have ceased fighting anything or anyone, even alcohol, for by this time sanity will have returned." Remember, in Step 2 we came to believe that a Power greater than ourselves could restore us to sanity. We believed, we decided, we acted, and now sanity has returned... "so long as we remain in a fit spiritual condition."

Whatever our problem has been—alcohol, drugs, food, gambling, other people—those things will still exist. They will still be in the world, but we will have a different attitude. They will no longer be a problem to us if we "remain in a fit spiritual condition" by working our Steps, especially this maintenance Step, Step 10.

A lot of us get impatient and want to make as much progress in our program and our lives as fast as we can. We get in a big hurry. *Most of our growth comes from working constantly and consistently,* a little bit of work every day rather than a whole lot of work for a short period of time. I think we get much more done if we steadily chip away and polish, rather than working in little spurts and then quitting. I think this is what Step 10 is for. We tend to work really hard on ourselves in a crisis, and when the crisis is over, we quit and rest. Step 10 is the Step that tells us how to live "one day at a time."

The quality of our lives is up to us. Step 10 also gives us a lot of responsibility. It's as if by working the first nine Steps, we have grown up, and now that we have the tools to change, whatever happens is our responsibility. We can't blame it on anybody else: it's not his fault, it's not her fault, it's not God's fault. Since it's our responsibility, we can change it. This seems like an awesome responsibility. Remember, though: *when it's someone else's fault, there is nothing we can do, but when it is ours, we are free—free to make it right.*

Instead of asking like we used to, "What did they do to me?" we can now ask "What did I do?" or "How is my thinking wrong?" We can get the answer by using the tools we have in Step 10. Regardless of other people's actions, we can change our reactions or choose not react at all. We no longer have to be victims, because now we have the tools to be responsible for ourselves. We can become adults.

Every once in a while, we're going to make a mistake and get into trouble, but if we get good at working Step 10, we're going to be able to catch ourselves quickly.

Step 5 said we were going to have a spiritual experience, and there has not been any update until we get here to Step 10. Now it says this: "You have entered the world of the spirit." This is powerful.

On Step 10, when we realize something is wrong, we can refer to our Step 4 inventory columns for understanding. We can say to ourselves, "I can't change things that appear in Columns 1 and 2, and I gave Column 3 to God. So when I'm in a problem, when I have a symptom or an uncomfortable feeling, I do a little inventory and ask myself, Am I self-seeking? Am I frightened? Am I selfish? Am I being inconsiderate? Am I being dishonest? This is the only way we can work this Step, because we can't do anything about the things we would have listed in Columns 1 through 3, but we can do something about the things in Column 4.

You can look at your Step 4 sheet and say this:

Column 1: Other people control this.

Column 2: This is still about others.

Column 3: God controls what's in this column.

Column 4: Here is my job!

All the things we need are already within us. God is within us, so we have all the courage and love and tolerance and patience we need, but all those positive qualities have been obscured by all the negative things we've been generating. We find out that when we get rid of the negative things, the good characteristics we want just naturally come out. The Big Book says "We will find that we have tapped an unsuspected inner resource of strength." (p. 570)

Love, courage, tolerance, patience—these are powerful things we can use in our lives. Step 10 is there to nurture them. They are unlimited, and as we practice them daily, we find they continue to grow.

Many people seem to fall into the trap of overloading their days with the problems of yesterday and tomorrow. We must remember that we are given strength for one day—and when we overload that day, it causes us great problems. We can see that Step 10 will guide us to an efficient use of our daily strength, and we will learn to live one day at a time.

The excitement of recovery is that it goes on forever. A person who is in a growth pattern can look back on his life every so often, and see that he is living in a world he didn't live in even a year before.

Tapping the Inner Resource

When I let go of the problem, I do not solve the problem, but I free myself for other things. I can go on with my life and forget about that problem. After a period of time, when I have given up wrestling with it and turned it over to God, the right answer will come.

Step 11: Sought through prayer and meditation to improve our conscious contact with God as we understood Him, *praying only for knowledge of His will for us and the power to carry that out.*

Step 11 is the culmination of all the other Steps. We have taken all the other Steps to lead us to this Step.

Step 1 had to be taken so we could take Step 2—because we couldn't see the solution until we understood the problem. These two Steps gave us what we needed to make a decision. The decision was Step 3: to turn our will and our lives over to the care of God *as we understood Him.* The decision was an important turning point.

Next we had to carry out the decision. There were certain things that blocked us from God, and we could not get on with turning our will and our lives over to the care of God until we removed those things that were blocking us. Therefore we took the action Steps: Steps 4, 5, 6, 7, 8, 9 and then 10, which is the continuation of Steps 4-9.

As a result of the actions of Steps 4-10, we removed the things that were blocking us from God. Now we can *carry out* the decision we made in Step 3 of turning our will and our lives over to the care of God as we understood Him. Through prayer and meditation, we can receive God's will for us and the power to carry it out. If we can do that, we will have carried out the decision that we made in Step 3. Steps 3 and 11 are the pillars of the Steps. We could say that the Steps have two crucial points: the turning over of our will in Step 3 and the receiving of God's will in Step 11.

This amounts to changing the direction of a human life. This is not to say the direction can be changed by these two Steps alone, because the others are necessary before we can complete these two.

When we change the direction of a life, we change the life. We said in Step 3 we were willing to turn our direction over to God, who had always been there even when we were blocked from Him. Our lives will have become different as a result of this

OUR WILL INTERACTS WITH GOD'S WILL

In Step 3:	In Step 11:
We ***give up*** our directions.	We ***receive*** God's directions.
We turn our will and our lives over ***to*** God as we understand Him	We receive God's will in our lives, and the power to carry it out ***from*** God as we understand Him.

process. Anyone who can begin to use Step 11 effectively has had a spiritual awakening. He or she has "tapped that unsuspected inner resource" of strength. (Big Book, pp. 569-570) This shows the Steps have worked for this person. After that will come the twelfth and final Step, which tells us to take the message to other people.

Step 11 takes a lot of work. First, it takes the work of the first ten Steps, and then it takes continuous practice over a long period of time.

There have been lots and lots of books written over the years by spiritual scholars about the subjects of prayer and meditation, but much of this writing has been over the heads of the people who really needed it. I love the way Bill W. has packed such a simple and complete program for spiritual living into so few words: pages 86, 87 and a little of page 88 in the Big Book. Bill does this so masterfully in these pages that I think surely he was guided in doing it. He didn't have a great spiritual background at this time. He had just been sober a few years himself and was struggling with his own spiritual life.

When Bill begins his discussion on the top of page 86, he says, "It would be easy to be vague about this matter." It seems obvious to me he means that he wishes he could escape this responsibility of writing something about prayer and meditation for a group of people who he knows are spiritually bankrupt. At this point he didn't know a lot about spirituality himself. This is probably one of the greatest miracles of the Big Book. The fact that Bill was *not* an expert in the field of prayer and meditation was probably a blessing. *He had to keep it simple, and he did.*

Since Bill didn't have the capacity to write like a great expert in spiritual things, he laid out a beautiful, simple daily exercise. This "spiritual kindergarten" can take anyone from wherever he is in his spiritual life, and show him how to develop a life of prayer and meditation.

Bill calls his daily exercises "some definite and valuable suggestions." He writes on meditation first, and then comes back to prayer. I call these the "Four Pillars of Prayer and Meditation":

1) Night
2) Morning
3) Indecision
4) Prayer

Let's look at these "valuable suggestions" in the order Bill laid them out:

p.m. *Night* relates to what we do at night. It is a nightly review. I think every person who's trying to develop a spiritual life should stop at night for this nightly review. One effective thing about a nightly review is that it gives evidence of what we have on hand. We have fresh in our minds what has taken place that day. Our future is unknown, but we have current evidence of what happened today.

As we've said, our thinking is our life, and we can look at today and see what the results of our thinking have been for today. As we do this every day, we can see things we need to change. We can see *each day* that we have, and will always have, two forces in our lives: self-will and God's will. Each night we can check to see how God's direction is growing in our lives.

Some days we'll find that self-will has caused us problems, and some days we'll see that God's will has been working in our lives. *No* day are we ever going to be perfect, and *no* day are we going to be completely on one side or the other. If we neglect to do this little nightly review, we're not going to know where we are, and the chances are we're going to forget where we came from, and where we're going.

These three things are very important in the business of living: *knowing where we came from, knowing where we are now, and knowing where we are going.* The nightly review allows us to keep up with these on a daily basis.

If we do the nightly review, and do it honestly, we'll see things we need to work on. We know we are never going to be perfect, but we will continue to make progress and to stay on the road we want to be on. Practicing this one "valuable suggestion" alone would change our lives completely, but we want to look at all four suggestions put together into a day.

a.m.

Morning deals with what we do in the morning. When we get up in the morning, we ask God to direct our lives that day. This is not going back and making the decision of Step 3 every day. We do this instead *to remind ourselves of our commitment each day.*

Most people get up each morning and prepare to meet the material world. We take a shower, brush our teeth, shave or put on make-up, fix our hair, dress carefully and thoughtfully, eat breakfast to nourish our physical bodies, lock our houses to protect our material possessions—and rush off and have turmoil and confusion in our lives all day. I wonder how much better, how much greater, our lives could be if we spent as much time preparing our minds each day as we spend preparing our clothes.

I know how well my car would run if I treated it with the same neglect that I do my mind. It wouldn't get me across town! I would never go without changing the oil or doing what needs to be done to keep that car going. We often don't take the same care with our lives.

If we simply ask God to direct our thinking in the morning, we will be more mindful of His directions all day. If we ask God to keep our thinking free from wrong motives, we can live better lives, tapping into this "inner resource" of strength each day. God can direct our lives in many ways that we are incapable of. We can only see so far; through *our* vision we cannot see the things that lie ahead. We know from the experience of traveling on self-will how *we* can direct our lives into a lot of catastrophes!

I love the passage in the Bible that says, "Thou shalt not be afraid of the terror by night; nor for the arrow that flieth by day; nor for the pestilence that walketh in the darkness; nor for the destruction that wasteth at noonday." (Psalms 91:5-6) Can you imagine being out in a field with thousands of arrows coming at you? *God can direct us through those arrows.* We can't. God can direct us through "arrows" and "pestilence"!

As we practice the nightly review and the morning meditation, we will become more skilled at them. These things will become the pillars of our day. We are only talking about a few minutes at night and a few minutes in the morning given to our spiritual health. Think what our lives would be like if we practiced this, if we spent five minutes at night reviewing and five minutes in the morning asking God to direct our lives through the "arrows." We would have twenty-three hours and fifty minutes to mess up and to run the show ourselves, but we would still be a lot better off. Most people think of prayer and meditation taking hours and hours of sitting around, but we are talking about a few minutes in the morning and a few minutes at night. Most of us are active people, and this is a simple thing that we can put into our lives without a lot of difficulty. It will give us strength to live by.

The third "valuable suggestion" deals with *indecision*. We all face indecision because we don't always have the knowledge or the understanding or the capacity to handle things that come up throughout the day. If we could just realize and accept the fact that we are human, we'd be in a good place to start handling decisions. It's all right not to know everything. Most of us allow ourselves to get frustrated because we feel we should know how to deal with everything and how to answer every question that comes along.

We have to realize the limitations we have. Human life is so short; we are here on earth for such a comparatively short period of time that it's impossible for us to know any significant part of what there is to know. At the same time, we have to believe that even though we are here for a short period of time, we are here to play a certain role and we have been equipped with enough information and ability to do it. If we can accept our role, and realize we're going to run into things in our lives that we don't understand or have any answer for, then we can turn these things over to God and ask for right and orderly directions.

I realize that God probably has a million answers to every problem I have. Since He can see all and knows all, He can direct my life through and around these things. He also has a covenant with me: He has given me self-will, and He will allow me to struggle on the basis of this self-will when I insist. When I realize this is happening, if I choose to, I can turn the problem over to God, relax, *take it easy, and not struggle.*

I can turn any indecision over to God and go on with my life. I have to realize it when I don't have the answer to a problem. I have to admit it and turn it over to God, and I will become free of the frustration. I still haven't solved the problem, but as long as I am wrestling with indecision, I can't solve that problem or handle anything else in my life! The confusion will have jammed my computer, and I won't be able to do anything else.

When I let go of the problem, I do not solve the problem, but I free myself for other things. I can go on with my life and forget about that problem. After a period of time, when I have given up wrestling with it and turned it over to God, the right answer will come. Sometimes the directions, the answers, will come from within me. A lot of times they will come from other people. This should make me more mindful that God is within other people, regardless of who they are. I used to have a big problem trying to select the people that I was willing to listen to very carefully. I wanted to listen to only "knowledgeable" people, but I have realized that God speaks through all kinds of people.

Sometimes the answer seems to come from within me. The Big Book says, "What used to be the hunch or the occasional inspiration gradually becomes a working part of the mind." (p. 87) We've all had hunches, but we've found that we really can't live on hunches—they come when they want to and go when they want to. They are not reliable. The Big Book says that if we keep practicing this program, they will gradually become a working part of our minds.

If we practice the program, we can live successfully. We won't have all the answers, but with this tool we can get any answer we need. We don't have to walk around with all the answers in our little heads. Remember, we weren't created to be self-sufficient. God did not make one of us to be self-sufficient. We were made to rely on God and on each other. As we learn to turn things over and receive God's directions, this principle is demonstrated very powerfully.

The fourth "valuable suggestion" deals with *prayer.* Most people who are having problems in their lives have an ineffective prayer life. If you are a spiritual giant, I guess you could say it is because your prayer life is healthy. But if you are experiencing tough going in your spiritual life, it is because of ineffective prayer. So this suggestion deals with effective prayer.

In my troubled life, I wasted all my prayer time telling God what I wanted. *I couldn't effectively use prayer to get directions because I used my prayers to give directions!* Prayer is meant to be where we receive our directions, but I used my whole prayer life directing God, telling him what to do. All that time, I needed Him to tell me what to do. It is very hard to switch one hundred eighty degrees, and go from directing God to Him directing you. We are people who have lost our direction in life, and the main

> **I ONCE WAS LOST,**
> **BUT NOW AM FOUND.**
>
> *Amazing Grace*

thing we need is God's directions.

Step 11 says that we pray *only* (notice this little word) "for the knowledge of His will for us and the power to carry that out." We often hear this word "only" read over so fast that we don't notice it, but the instruction is very specific. We are talking about priorities. Other priorities in our lives may change, but to one who has been lost, the number one priority for the rest of his life is God's direction. If God directs our lives, and we have the power to carry out His direction, we will find we are able to take care of most of the other things in life we've been asking Him for.

I always used God to get me out of trouble, but I've found out in twenty-seven years of asking Him to direct my life that I didn't *need* to ask Him to get me out of trouble. I realized that *God's will for me is always good.* I also realized that *God's direction has always been in my life,* but, instead of using it to carry out His will, I did *my* will and used His to put myself down and make myself feel bad with guilt and remorse. Instead of using it in a positive way, I used it in a negative way. Later, when I found out what it was, I recognized it.

All my life, when I was about to do something, I knew whether it was right or wrong. For example, I never told a lie that I didn't know was a lie. You don't really "slip" and do that kind of thing. God's direction may have seemed small or it may have seemed inadequate, but Step 11 is about our awakening to God's direction, allowing it to come alive in our lives. As we practice these suggestions and tap the "inner resource," we'll come to rely on God's direction, and we'll find that Step 11 has become the force of our lives.

What we are talking about is each person developing his own healthy prayer life. Everyone who is willing to work at this can, in a short period of time, begin to feel the results of having a prayer life.

For a long time my prayers were ineffective, but I didn't realize why. It was because instead of praying for God's direction, my prayers were like letters to Santa Claus: "God, do this" and "God, do that." Sometimes my prayers were answered, and often I didn't recognize they had been. After a while, I sort of gave up on the whole thing.

We need to remember to pray as if it all depended on God and work as if it all depended on us.

Once we simplify our prayers and ask only for God's directions and the power to carry them out, once we see God's directions throughout the day and act on them, we will see God working in our lives more and more each day.

A passerby saw St. Francis tending a garden. He said, "You must have prayed very hard, Francis, for things to grow so well." Francis said, "Yes, and every time I prayed, I picked up my hoe."

Somebody told me once that when you pray for potatoes, the next thing you do is go get a spade and start digging. You don't sit on the porch and wait for something to start happening. We have to get involved, because we are promised that God will give us directions and the power to carry them out. It's not magic. We still have to put the work into it. We have to get out there and get these things done.

Developing a healthy prayer life takes time. We are people who have been lost, and we have to develop new prayer habits that will give us a simple expression of God's will in our lives each day. We will find that with God directing our lives, we won't have to use prayer as we once did to get us out of trouble. We'll be able to handle our own business, even financial, as we never have been before.

In the closing paragraph on page 87, Bill gives us what I call some "mini-suggestions":

- If circumstances warrant, we ask our wives or friends to join us in morning meditation.
- If we belong to a religious denomination which requires a definite morning devotion, we attend to that also.
- We sometimes select and memorize a few set prayers which emphasize the principles we have been discussing.
- There are many helpful books also.

He goes on to advise us that suggestions from a priest, minister, or rabbi may be helpful to us. We may want to discipline ourselves to make these suggestions part of our program of recovery.

It is quite a miracle to take a life that has been unmanageable for perhaps ten or fifteen years and, by chipping away day in and day out with this spiritual program, to turn that life around. Once we start seeing the change, the benefits of this work, we will no longer have to *make* ourselves work it—we will *want* to.

This is a very practical program; we don't have to be in any particular place or any particular position or posture to ask for our directions—that is, to say our prayers. This is not a religious program. There is no ritual involved. We can do it in the shower, in our car, anywhere we are. With God directing our lives, we will be more efficient than we were when we were burning up energy running on self-will. (Big Book, p. 88) As the days go by, we will notice that we are accomplishing more things, and our sense of self-worth will naturally go up. This is what it's all about.

I heard a guy say once that the brain, though a small organ, burns a lot of energy: every fourth breath we breathe is used by the brain. When we work against the will of God, it wears us out. Our whole bodies may be tired, and yet we may not have accomplished a thing.

I think God placed each and every one of us here on earth for a purpose, and I think the happiest and most efficient we're going to be is when we're doing what we're supposed to be doing. *We don't know what we are supposed to be doing; only God knows the purpose He put us here for.* Until we have exhausted self-will, He can't use us for the purpose we were created and put here for. If we have our directions from God, we can do what we are supposed to be doing, and we will be happy with it. We won't need what other people have to be happy. We will know that what we need is God's directions and the power to carry them out.

We don't always know *how* we're going to carry out God's directions. When we started writing this book, somebody said, "How are you going to do it?" I said, "I don't know."

Recently I've been remodeling and moving into a new treatment center, and it seems everybody who has come by has asked the same question: "Man, where did you get all this money?" I say, "What money? I don't have any money. There are a whole lot of people working together. There is not as much money here as it looks like. All of us have scuffled around here for this and that, and it just came together."

I believe that if I show up every day and put my part in, and what we're doing is good and is God's will, it is going to work out. I have never seen it fail! I started out down at Serenity House with $300. I had a building, some old beds, fifteen folding chairs and two desks. In six weeks we had mattresses, bedding, pots and pans, televisions, things that people had given us or helped us get. We even had curtains on the windows. We had the place looking good in six weeks, and we had people in treatment. We had to prop the oven door closed with a stick to get the bread to brown, but that was okay!

One day we were sitting there at the table. We had had some beans and a pan of cornbread for lunch, and the guys were leaned back smoking cigarettes and laughing and joking. It came to me, "I don't know what's so funny: there's nothing back there for dinner." But when dinnertime came, we had something. We were getting one meal at a time.

So *now* when people ask me about something—"How is that going to work out?"—I think, "If I knew how it was going to work out, I would be God, but it isn't anything compared to the things I've already seen work out." Some of the things we have done can't be done! The trick is to keep showing up, keep being responsible, and keep doing what you're supposed to do.

It's like that story about the little woodpecker who was pecking on this great big old oak tree when lightning struck it and knocked it flat to the ground. All the other woodpeckers flew up to him and asked, "How in the world did you do that?" He said, "Well, I showed up where I was supposed to be and did what I was supposed to do, and God did the rest." I've felt like that little woodpecker a lot of times.

I also like the story of David the little shepherd boy and the giant Goliath. They asked David how he was planning to take on the giant. They pointed out to David that Goliath had armor, swords, spears, and all manner of weapons, and that David only had some stones and a slingshot—and that Goliath was so big and David was so little. David told them a story. He said, "When I was tending my sheep in the field, a lion came among my flock." David said (and this is what I consider to be the key), *"I went out* and God delivered him unto me." Then he said, *"I will go down into the valley* and He will deliver Goliath unto me." The important thing here, I think, is that David is *not trying to control outcomes.* He knows all he has to do is *do his part.* He doesn't have to wait until he figures out how God is going to do *His* part; he just has to go ahead and go where he is supposed to go and do what he is supposed to do, and leave the outcome to God. The secret here is in David's faith—"I will go out."

This is all we're talking about when we ask for God's directions in our lives and the power to carry them out. We want the ability, the faith, to say "I will go out" and face life without knowing what the results will be. We need the courage to go out and do what we can, as far as we can see that day, and let go of the outcomes. We can have this for the asking!

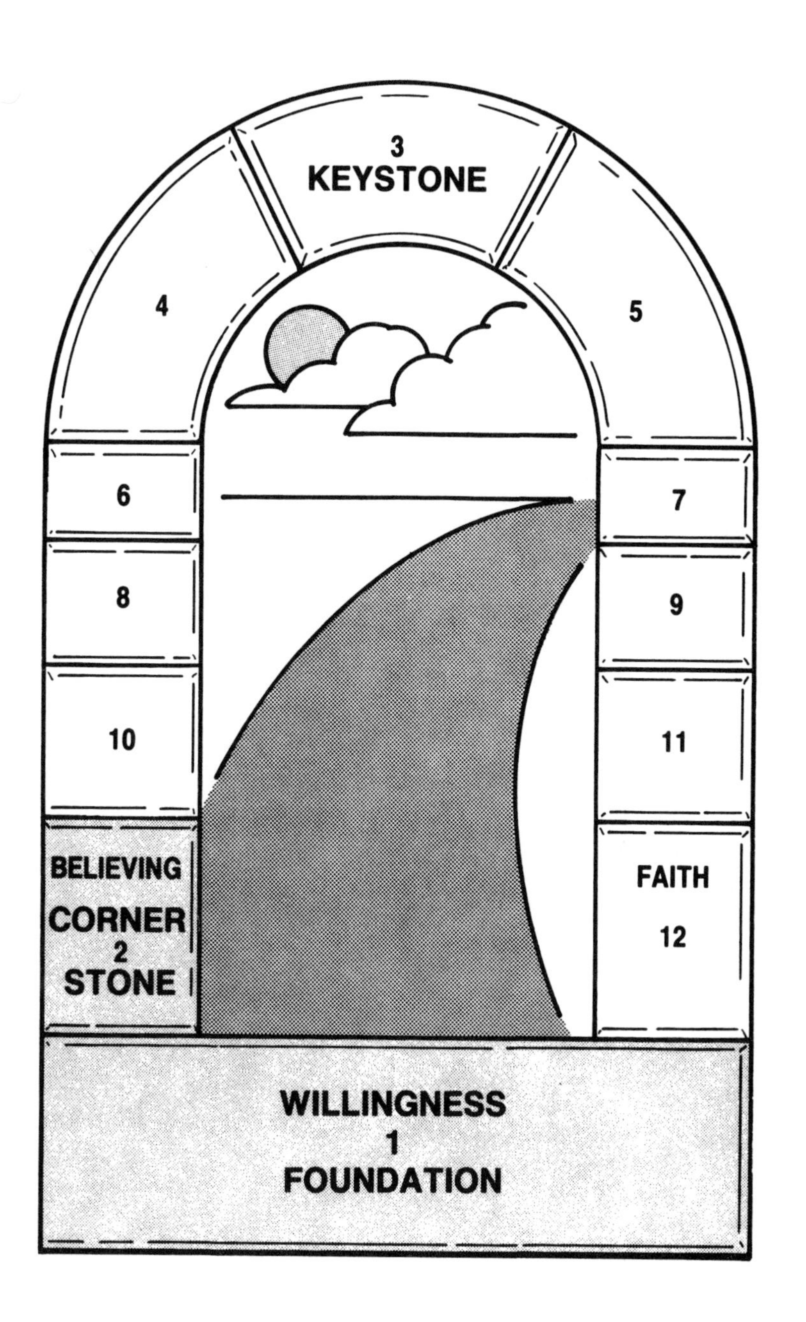

"...the arch through which we passed to freedom."

Carrying the Message

We can now sit down with another individual who has a problem similar to our own and convey an understanding that no one else can. We can say to him or to her, "I've been there." Because of our experience we can cross barriers of race, religion, and every other kind, and we can understand each other in a very special and meaningful way.

Step 12: Having had a spiritual awakening as the result of these Steps, we tried to carry this message to others, and to practice these principles in all our affairs.

Step 12 gives us a guarantee—a promise that if we take the first eleven Steps, we will have a spiritual awakening. The result of working these Steps is just that: a spiritual awakening. We have tapped the "unsuspected inner resource" of strength by working these Steps, and our spirit is awakened. (Big Book, pp. 569-570)

Now we carry this message to others: "I have tapped an inner resource with the first eleven Steps, and if you have a problem in your life and you would like to tap your inner resource, this is the way you can do it. It has worked for me."

This is all the message is. It is very simple: *here is a program that works.*

Throughout the Big Book, Bill talks about a "sudden spiritual experience" which effected his recovery and influenced his writing and the focus of the book. Later on, when they were putting out the second edition, a lot of people asked him not to emphasize his sudden spiritual experience because they thought many people might feel they would have to have the same type of spiritual experience in order to recover. So he changed the term to "spiritual awakening." The distinction is that a "spiritual experience" happens suddenly, and a "spiritual awakening" happens more gradually. It doesn't matter which we have (far more people have the gradual kind of spiritual awakening), but we are *promised* that if we work these Steps, we will become spiritually awakened.

I believe there are as many different experiences of spiritual awakening as there are people. It is a very personal thing. God knows that no two people are alike. Each person is going to have a unique spiritual experience or a unique spiritual awakening that will fit his or her particular life. Each one will be like no other, but they all will have something in common: *we will be able to think, believe, and feel things that we couldn't before.* We will be able to do things we couldn't do on our own strength. We can receive God's directions in our lives; we have had a spiritual awakening.

This is what we carry to other people. Remember that we said if we can believe in Step 2, and decide in Step 3 and act in Steps 4, 5, 6, 7, 8, and 9, we will get the Promises in Step 9 and results in Step 10, and the results of prayer and meditation in Step 11.

Now we know. We are people who have faith. We have seen the program work for us, and those of us who know from our own experience that it works can go to the new person and help him or her come to believe. Our faith and our knowledge can enable him to believe. We have to be careful, though, because we can't make him willing. He has to become willing on his own, through his problem. If he has had enough of what he has been experiencing, and he is willing to let go of it, then we can step in and say, "This is what worked for me!"

A lot of times we try to get people to believe who are not willing yet. This is something the individual has to do on his own; he has to go through his own suffering to become willing to change.

This is our message, and it is simple. Our responsibility is to carry the message–what others do with it is not our responsibility. Recovery comes through a vital spiritual experience as a result of these Steps. I think this is the only way to recovery. Our job is not someone else's recovery; our job is simply to carry the message. When you look at it, it seems like a small, insignificant thing we are asked to do: not to promote the recovery, not to effect the recovery, but to carry the recovery message.

I think sometimes we miss the boat. We want to carry the message and also carry out the message. Then when the person doesn't recover or doesn't respond to the message, we assume responsibility. We need to remember that the recovery comes through the message, through the power of the Steps, and not through the messenger. Our job is simply to tell people.

The twelfth Step is about faith. When we talk to a new person we don't talk about anything we "believe," we talk about what we have known through experience. We talk about facts that have brought results in our lives. Remember where he is, though. He can't sit there and get our faith. It is often frustrating because we wish that he knew what we know, that we could just give him the knowledge we have.

The new person has to start where we started. Sometimes it is helpful to remember how we thought in the beginning. He has to start wherever he is and go through the Steps on his own just as we did. One day he will know it works, and one day he can tell another person. This is the chain reaction that has taken place in the fifty years since the beginnings of this program in Alcoholics Anonymous.

Here is an irony that shows the power of God. We have taken the problem—whatever it was we were powerless over, whatever was destroying our self-worth, destroying our lives, giving us guilt and fear and shame, and making us feel like a zero—and finally become willing to let go of it. We have come to believe, have made a decision, and have taken the actions. Then after we have gotten God's direction in our lives, we come to the twelfth Step, and we find out the *thing that seemed the worst,* that we hated the most, *is really the jewel of our life.* In the end it is the only thing we have enough understanding of to offer to the rest of the world.

We can now sit down with another person who has a problem similar to our own and convey an understanding that no one else can. We can say to him or to her, "I've been there." Because of our experience we can cross barriers of race, religion and every other kind, and we can understand each other in a very special and meaningful way.

There are often people we want to help but can't because we don't get to choose. I'm glad we don't have the right to choose who we will help, because I might not have been chosen. It is still the miracle of our programs that we can come together as we do and share our experience, strength, and hope, and watch each other get well.

One of the hardest situations we face is with our family members. We would all like to "save" the members of our families, but often we can't. I had one brother, and he was an alcoholic. I sobered up one March, and he died right after Christmas the same year. He was thirty-seven years old. I was thirty-four. He never saw me after I got sober. I've been able to help with a lot of people since then, but I never was given the opportunity to help my brother. There are a lot of things I can't figure out; this is one of them.

A guy who helped me get sober was drunk six weeks after we got out of the hospital, and he was killed in a car wreck drunk ten years later. At the time we were together in the hospital, he was very interested in the program and trying to get me interested in it. I don't understand God's will. Some of us are chosen through our problem, and our recovery teaches us the program of action to recover. Each time a person gets well through this program, he or she has the responsibility to take the message to other people who still suffer in the same situation.

In all the other Steps, Steps 1 through 11, we have received something, all culminating in Step 11. But in Step 12 we are told to give it all away. So eleven Steps give to us and one we give away. We can see the power of what Jesus meant when he said that it is more blessed to give than to receive! (Acts 20:35)

When I look back at my own life, I see that the first eleven Steps brought an amazing change in my life and gave me a spiritual experience. But when I look back over the past twenty-seven years of working with others I know I have grown far more from carrying the message than I grew through the first eleven Steps. This—Step 12—is the growth Step. It's what Jesus was talking about: the more I give what I have been given, the more I am blessed by God growing in my life. The more God grows in my life, the better off I am going to be.

At the end of Step 12, it says "to practice these principles in all our affairs." Throughout the Big Book, Bill W. refers to the Twelve Steps as "principles." In the foreword of *Twelve Steps and Twelve Traditions* he says, "The twelve Steps of Alcoholics Anonymous are a set of principles, spiritual in nature, which if practiced will expel the obsession to drink." I think the best word for principles is "laws." I think these are laws that have been created by something beyond man, and they are just as basic and unchanging as the law of gravity or the freezing point of water. Water always freezes at thirty-two degrees; we can depend on it. We can just as confidently depend on these laws that are within our Steps.

> **...that they might have life, and that they might have it more abundantly.**
>
> *John 10:10*

The Twelve Steps are a design for living. They are a set of principles (or laws or directions) that tell us how a human being should live. If we can live by these principles, we will be peaceful and content. We will be free from the things that used to enslave us and make our lives miserable.

We do have self-will—we can do what we want to do—or we can choose to live by these principles. I think the reason most people choose to live miserable lives indulging self-will is not because they are evil or bad or sinful or anything like that. I think they are just ignorant; they just don't know. But we can help other people because we know. We have been on both sides of these principles. We know what works, we know how it works, and this is the simple message we try to carry. These are the basic and unchanging principles we try to practice in all our affairs.

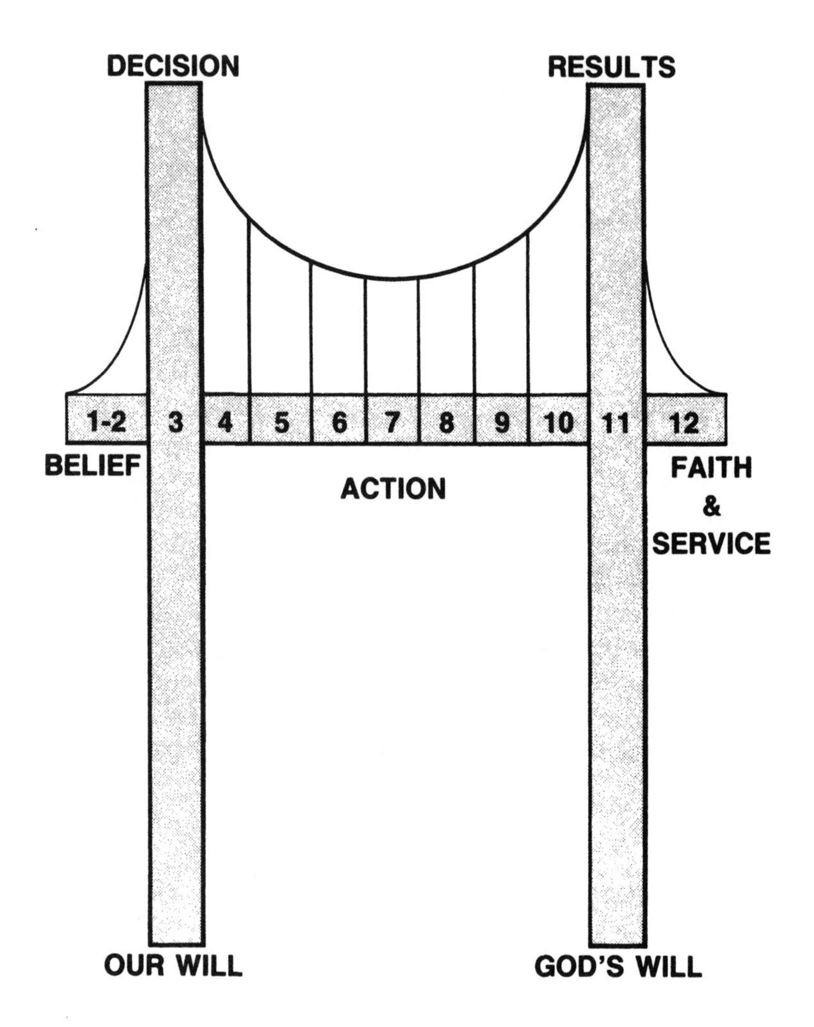

"...over the Bridge of Reason towards the desired shore of faith."

Appendix 1

What are the Principles?

Step 1: Admitting defeat, denying ourselves, getting willingness
Step 2: Believing
Step 3: Deciding, surrendering our will
Step 4: Examining ourselves, seeking the truth
Step 5: Sharing, asking for feedback, seeking the truth
Step 6: Getting willingness, changing
Step 7: Getting humility, changing
Step 8: Living with others
Step 9: Living with others, taking responsibility
Step 10: Continuing to grow, continuing to examine ourselves
Step 11: Continuing to grow, refining our spiritual growth
Step 12: Continuing to grow through giving to others

As the Big Book says, "We claim spiritual progress rather than spiritual perfection." (p. 60) "Progress" means growth. All growth is built on a foundation of willingness.

Appendix 2

Religious Beliefs

It would be very difficult for a person living in our time not to have been exposed to religious beliefs or concepts. Religion is simply man's collective concept of God. These concepts, formed by groups over a long period of time, have often been successful in bringing people to the point of a *personal* conception of the power called God. At the same time, the concepts have been confusing and detrimental to others. Religion has been used by different groups as a giant funnel to channel people into a personal conception of God. However, many people get wrapped up in beliefs and never find a personal concept or arrive at a point of faith.

These conceptions are usually initiated in a person's early development. Early conceptions, if they are to remain effective, must grow.

Examples: A parent six feet tall must look like a giant to a small child. A full scale bicycle will seem insurmountable. A two-story building is a skyscraper. God is an old man who watches and is sometimes used by the parent as a babysitter. He guards, scolds, and punishes.

We can see how a child's conception of his parent changes as he grows to the parent's height. The insurmountable bicycle is easily ridden. The two-story building no longer seems so high. Our conceptions of these things have grown as we have grown. But there seems to be a built-in system within many religions that discourages our conceptions of God from growing along with the other areas of our lives. *A person with adult problems and difficulties with a childish perception of the Power greater than himself may have a very hard time making a spiritual beginning on these problems.*

Childish conceptions need not be cast out, but simply set

aside. An adult conception of the source of Power that dominates our universe, that turns our planets, produces the sun, wind, rain and energy, may begin by simply believing.

Adapted with permission from *Recovery Dynamics*

Appendix 3

Self-Pity

Once a self-centered person is offended by another, the self-centered individual then resents his own position in life. This is self-resentment or self-pity. Resentment at self (along with resentment against others) is a major emotional problem. It is one of the most destructive emotional bad habits a person can have.

Resentment against self is almost always associated with resentments toward others. As soon as the person is offended and reacts with resentments towards others, he automatically directs the same deadly poison toward himself. This emotional bad habit can only lead to unhappiness and failure. The individual who persists in the overuse of self-pity sees everyone else as a success and himself as a failure. As a result, he constantly resents his position in life and feels put upon by all others.

The intensity of self-pity masks the individual's positive qualities—his assets and intellectual abilities. Such a person's goals become fantasies upon which he builds his life. The combination of these two, self-pity and fantasizing, then produces a state of non-activity and failure.

Constructive Use of Self-Pity

The constructive use of self-pity is God-given. A reaction that produces an action is a success mechanism. When one individual performs a task or a feat that bypasses another individual, the person who has been bypassed resents his own position. If resentment brings about an action to obtain a new goal, then it is a healthy use of self-resentment or self-pity.

Example: There are two houses on the block that need painting. One industrious fellow purchases paint, brushes and equipment and begins to paint his house. The occupant of the other house takes note of this activity, while rocking on his porch. Noticing the condition of his house, he, too, purchases paint and begins repainting. Then there are two houses painted, improving the entire community. This case illustrates the healthy use of self-pity. The second individual reacted with self-pity, and by not liking the condition of his house anymore, he took action.

We can see how the healthy instinct has propelled human beings since time began to produce constant change and development in our society. It is this reaction we have toward each other that makes us explore our intellectual abilities and produces progress in society.

Destructive Use of Self-Pity

The destructive use of self-pity can be seen when the God-given instinct fails to produce action, and proceeds to a stalemate of inaction.

Example: Two houses on the block need painting. One man purchases equipment and begins to paint. The other man, sitting on the porch in his rocking chair, notices the new project next door. He resents the man who is painting the house. He looks at his house but takes no action. He continues to rock on his porch, feeling sorry for himself, probably saying, "I don't have the money to paint my house," resulting in further resentment of the man of action next door. The level of self-pity deepens within him. As one emotional problem triggers others, this man of inactivity will constantly resent future projects initiated by his neighbor.

In these two examples we can see clearly that in one case, self-pity produced action; in the other case, self-pity produced inaction. Action is the key in a healthy response just as inaction produces unhealthy responses.

Self-Pity Relates to Self-Centeredness

It is obvious the role of self in self-centeredness—it is part of the term. The stronger the self-drive, the stronger the self-pity. The highly driven self-centered personality who directs his life and the lives of others is constantly in collision with people, places, and things. Self-centeredness is the root of all his collisions and resulting resentments. Such an individual is prone to self-pity and cannot fail to see himself as a failure and a loser.

The resentful, self-pitying person becomes a total reactor. His happiness and contentment are based on how others perform. He becomes a parasite as his happiness is tuned to the actions of others as they live their lives; when others don't respond to his whims, the self-pity or self-resentment becomes more deep-seated. We can see the impossibility of overcoming self-pity without removing self-will as we have done previously in Step 3.

We can see the vital role Step 3 plays in this particular emotional bad habit. Once self-will has been tempered or removed, the overuse of self-pity will disappear. The individual learns to accept his role in life and changes this pattern to respond with action. At this point, the destructive force of self-pity will become a constructive force used to obtain goals. Thus we find the recovering person to be a healthy individual who exercises his natural instinct to promote contentment and serenity along with healthy competitive progress.

Monitoring the Instinct in Step 10

Once this instinct has become a major problem in the life of an individual, its intensity should be monitored daily. Each feeling of self-pity should produce action. If action is not possible in a particular situation, self-pity should be dealt with as soon as possible because it only produces pain. Therefore, constant monitoring for self-pity must be done by the recovering person. The emotional bad habit of recalling old incidents of the past to relive self-pity must be eliminated. Positive responses must be developed to replace the old. "I can" must replace "I can't."

Adapted with permission from
Recovery Dynamics

Appendix 4

Extra Inventories

You may freely copy these forms for your use.

Review C

INSTRUCTIONS FOR COMPLETION

Instruction 1 — In dealing with resentments we set them on paper. We listed people, institutions, or principles with whom we are angry. (Complete column 1 from top to bottom. Do nothing on columns 2, 3, or 4 until column 1 is complete.)

Instruction 2 — We asked ourselves why we were angry. (Complete column 2 from top to bottom. Do nothing on columns 3 or 4 until column 2 is complete.)

Instruction 3 — On our grudge list we set opposite each name our injuries. Was it our self-esteem, our security, our ambitions, our personal or sex relations which had been interfered with? (Complete each column within column 3 going from top to bottom, starting with the Self-Esteem column and finishing with the Sexual Ambitions column. Do nothing on column 4 until column 3 is complete.)

Instruction 4 — (Referring to our list again.) Putting out of our minds the wrongs others had done, we resolutely looked for our own mistakes. Where had we been selfish, dishonest, self-seeking, and frightened and inconsiderate? (Asking ourselves the above questions, we complete each column within column 4.)

Instruction 5 — Reading from left to right we now see the resentment (column 1), the cause (column 2), the part of self that had been affected (column 3), and the exact nature of the defect within us that allowed the resentment to surface and block us off from God's will (column 4).

	COLUMN 1	COLUMN 2
	I'm resentful at:	The cause:
1		
2		
3		
4		
5		
6		
7		

Resentments

"SELF" COLUMN 3									COLUMN 4			
Affects My... (Which part of self caused the fear?)									What is the exact nature of my wrongs, faults, mistakes, defects, shortcomings:			
Social Instinct		Security Instinct		Sex Instinct		Ambitions						
Self-Esteem	Personal Relationships	Material	Emotional	Acceptable Sex Relations	Hidden Sex Relations	Social	Security	Sexual	Selfish	Dishonest	Self-Seeking Frightened	Incnsiderate

Review

INSTRUCTIONS FOR COMPLETION

Instruction 1 — In dealing with fears we set them on paper. We listed people, institutions, or principles with whom we were fearful. (Complete column 1 from top to bottom. Do nothing on columns 2, 3, or 4 until column 1 is complete.)

Instruction 2 — We asked ourselves why we have the fear. (Complete column 2 from top to bottom. Do nothing on columns 3 or 4 until column 2 is complete.)

Instruction 3 — What part of self caused the fear? Was it our self-esteem, our security, our ambitions, our personal or sex relations which had been interfered with? (Complete each column within column 3 going from top to bottom, starting with the Self-Esteem column and finishing with the Sexual Ambitions column. Do nothing on column 4 until column 3 is complete.)

Instruction 4 — (Referring to our list again.) Putting out of our minds the wrongs others had done, we resolutely looked for our own mistakes. Where had we been selfish, dishonest, self-seeking, and frightened and inconsiderate? (Asking ourselves the above questions, we complete each column within column 4.)

Instruction 5 — Reading from left to right we now see the fear (column 1), why we have the fear (column 2), the part of self that caused the fear (column 3), and the exact nature of the defect within us that allowed the fear to surface and block us off from God's will (column 4).

	COLUMN 1 I'm fearful of:	COLUMN 2 Why do I have the fear?
1		
2		
3		
4		
5		
6		
7		

Of Fears

"SELF" COLUMN 3									COLUMN 4			
Affects My... (Which part of self caused the fear?)									What is the exact nature of my wrongs, faults, mistakes, defects, shortcomings:			
Social Instinct		Security Instinct		Sex Instinct		Ambitions						
Self-Esteem	Personal Relationships	Material	Emotional	Acceptable Sex Relations	Hidden Sex Relations	Social	Security	Sexual	Selfish	Dishonest	Self-Seeking Frightened	Incnsiderate

Review Of Ou

INSTRUCTIONS FOR COMPLETION

Instruction 1 — We listed people we harmed. (Complete column 1 from top to bottom. Do nothing on columns 2, 3, or 4 until column 1 is complete.)

Instruction 2 — We asked ourselves what we did. (Complete column 2 from top to bottom. Do nothing on columns 3 or 4 until column 2 is complete.)

Instruction 3 — Was it our self-esteem, our security, our ambitions, our personal or sex relations which had been interfered with? (Complete each column within column 3 going from top to bottom, starting with the Self-Esteem column and finishing with the Sexual Ambitions column. Do nothing on column 4 until column 3 is complete.)

Instruction 4 — (Referring to our list again.) Putting out of our minds the wrongs others had done, we resolutely looked for our own mistakes. Where had we been selfish, dishonest, self-seeking, and frightened and inconsiderate? (Asking ourselves the above questions, we complete each column within column 4.)

Instruction 5 — Reading from left to right we now see the harm (column 1), what we did (column 2), the part of self that caused the harm (column 3), and the exact nature of the defect within us that allowed the harm to surface and block us off from God's will (column 4).

	COLUMN 1	COLUMN 2
	Who did I harm?	What did I do?
1		
2		
3		
4		
5		
6		
7		

Own Sex Conduct

"SELF" COLUMN 3									COLUMN 4			
Affects My... (Which part of self caused the harm?)									What is the exact nature of my wrongs, faults, mistakes, defects, shortcomings:			
Social Instinct		Security Instinct		Sex Instinct		Ambitions						
Self-Esteem	Personal Relationships	Maierial	Emotional	Acceptable Sex Relations	Hidden Sex Relations	Social	Security	Sexual	Selfish	Dishonest	Self-Seeking Frightened	Incnsiderate

People I

INSTRUCTIONS FOR COMPLETION

List the people you have harmed in any way.
A. Listing from top to bottom.
B. List what you did.
C. What part of self caused you the harm? (Column 3)
D. What character defect was involved? (Column 4)

	COLUMN 1	COLUMN 2
	Whom did I hurt?	What did I do?
1		
2		
3		
4		
5		
6		
7		

Have Harmed

"SELF" COLUMN 3									COLUMN 4			
Affects My... (Which part of self caused the harm?)									What is the exact nature of my wrongs, faults, mistakes, defects, shortcomings:			
Social Instinct		Security Instinct		Sex Instinct		Ambitions						
Self-Esteem	Personal Relationships	Material	Emotional	Acceptable Sex Relations	Hidden Sex Relations	Social	Security	Sexual	Selfish	Dishonest	Self-Seeking Frightened	Incnsiderate

Afterword

Joe Reminisces About the Beginning of Big Book Studies

When we started the Step meeting, it didn't have any plan or structure to it. At that time we had two meetings here: we had a speaker meeting, and what we called a Twelve-Step discussion meeting. We basically sat around and discussed the Steps with new people in the program. There were only a few people, and nobody knew much about the Steps. Our meeting was on Tuesday night, and a lot of Tuesday nights I would go and nobody would show up.

After a few years our group got going a little better, and some people asked me, "Why don't you take a Step and explain it to us?" I had about two years in the program at this time, and I was an old hand! I really didn't know anything either, but since they asked me, I studied it so I could talk to them about it and we could discuss it. Well, after we had been going three or four years, we had about five or six people who knew the Steps, and I said, "Let's switch this to a discussion meeting." But one of the members, named Esther S., said, "You're doing alright. Just keep doing what you are doing." So that's the way we got this meeting started.

Then we moved to the old Serenity House in 1973. The group would rent the meeting room there on Saturday night. People in other groups found out what we were doing and started coming. I think we had the meeting there from 1973 until 1983, when we bought Wolfe Street. During those years it grew until we didn't have the physical space. Sometimes we'd have a hundred people in that house on Monday night. People would say, "I'd really like to come to that meeting, but I can't get in." When we moved to Wolfe Street, the meeting really took off.

We take twelve weeks to work through the Steps, with two weeks on Step 4-and then we start over and do it all again. There are 250 to 300 people there every Monday night. They come from all the different Twelve-Step groups.

I met Charlie P. in 1973. It was during the time I was studying the Big Book. I had a good program personally, and I could work with a person one-on-one, but I didn't have effective skills to work with a large group of people. This is what I went back into the Big Book for. I met Charlie at an Al-Anon meeting here in Little Rock in 1973. He was at the Roadway Inn speaking at an Al-Anon conference. We started talking, and I found out he had a greater interest in the Big Book than anybody I knew. So we started studying together, and it was nice to have someone to talk to who was as interested as I was in studying it. We would make notes on our own, and get together and compare notes, and we began to find the underlying plan of the Big Book.

We would meet at conferences and put the pieces together like a puzzle. One day we were in a hotel room at a conference, and Charlie asked me if another guy, named Tony, could sit in. I felt kind of funny about it, like the guy was barging in, but he sat in that night, and the next time some more guys sat in, and soon every time we'd go to one of these local conferences like Hot Springs or Tulsa or Eufaula or anywhere, we'd end up having an informal meeting on the Steps in one of the hotel rooms. We were never on the program or anything; it just got to be expected.

Then one time in 1974 I was mopping the floor (somebody had mopped it, and of course hadn't done it well enough to suit me), and the phone rang. It was the organizer of the Arkansas state conference in Eureka Springs. He told me the Sunday morning speaker had had to back out, and he asked if I would speak. I said, "Sure, I'll take care of it," and went back to my mopping. Then I thought, "What in the world have I done? I can't do that!"

Sure enough, I went and gave the talk. that was the first conference I ever spoke at. The scheduled speaker had gotten drunk after twelve years of recovery.

I started getting invited to speak at conferences. Charlie and

I kept on studying the Big Book, and between 1974 and 1983 I spoke at about seventy-five conferences a year. Charlie and I would do four or five Big Book Studies a year. Then, in 1980, at the international convention, Wesley gave away some of our tapes as door prizes. They went to every state, and some of them went overseas. This is how our Big Book tapes got their exposure.

Charlie and I began to be asked to do Big Book Studies, and as we did, I became less and less involved in conference and convention speaking because my time was booked so far ahead.

I feel like the Big Book Study gives me a chance to accomplish more; I find it more rewarding. I went all over this country and Canada during that period of time–and it was quite an experience–but I haven't found anything as rewarding as giving the Big Book Studies. This year (1989), Charlie and I did thirty-three Big Book Studies; last year we did thirty-six.

I put this book (a copy of the Big Book) in a cover in 1986, and every time I've gone to a different place to do a Big Book Study I've written the name of the place on the next page. My last entry is on page 99, and there are twenty pages in the Big Book before you get to page one.

The first entry on the first empty page is Baton Rouge, Louisiana, September, 1986. Then come Austin, Texas–Braden, Minnesota–Albuquerque, New Mexico–Pompano Beach, Florida–Lexington, Kentucky–Nassau, Bahamas–Joe Wheeler State Park, Alabama–Plano, Texas–Ft. Smith, Arkansas–Levelland, Texas– Pittsburgh, Pennsylvania--Lafayette, Louisiana–Houma, Louisiana–Phoenix, Arizona--Toronto–Terre Haute, Indiana–Port Arthur, Texas–Omaha, Nebraska–Eureka Springs, Arkansas–Yukon, Oklahoma–Memphis, Tennessee–Kansas City, Missouri–Abilene, Texas--Barstow, California–Hardwick, Georgia–Jackson, Tennessee-Yakima, Washington –Texas Department of Corrections, Houston, Texas–Houston O.A.–Charleston, South Carolina–Hot Springs, Arkansas–New Orleans, Louisiana–Des Moines, Iowa–Alliston, Ontario–Sacramento, California –Wheeling, West Virginia–Burlington, Vermont– West Palm Beach, Florida–Denton, Texas...

We started doing Big Book Studies in 1977, and these are some of the places we've done them since I started logging them in this book in 1986.

The Word from Joe

'It's gonna be okay'

Friday, November 2, 2007

LITTLE ROCK — LIFE IS STRANGE. That's not an original observation, since life keeps demonstrating just how strange it is. Consider the life and saving times of Joseph Daniel McQuany, 1928-2007. Mr. McQuany, who became much better known as just Joe around Little Rock, was one of the most successful people we've ever heard of.

Joe touched, indeed transformed, the lives of who knows how many tens of thousands in his city, state, country and beyond. He started an enterprise on a shoestring or less-a $330 grant and some charitable donations-that grew into a publishing company, traveling mission, growing institution, and, most important, a blessing.

The secret of his success? "If I hadn't been an alcoholic," he confided to one of the many groups he addressed, "I probably would have amounted to nothing."

And all because one day back in 1962, Joe McQuany decided he'd get sober. In those days, he'd recall, white men trying to get on the wagon could find a treatment program, black men were sent to the State Hospital-aka the Nut House in the patois of the times-and as for women alcoholics, the only place for them was jail.

Once detoxed, Joe McQuany knew he'd have to find some way to stay sober. His way was Alcoholics Anonymous, even though, in 1962, as a black man he would be left out of the social bonding that's such an important if informal part of its program. No matter. He had the Twelve Steps, AA's version of the Ten Commandments, and the Big Book. A testament and a faith. What more does a natural leader need? Build on it and the people will come.

Soon the man was organizing AA groups himself. He was a whiz at it. Not only because he'd been there and knew the cravings and excuses, the real desperation and false exhilaration of it all, but maybe because to save himself he had to save others.

JOE McQUANY wound up founding an offshoot of AA himself. He called his program Serenity House before it had a house-an old one on Broadway in Little Rock. As his program grew, he moved it to larger and larger quarters.

Serenity House became Serenity Park-an extended-care sanctuary for all, black or white, penniless or professional, who needed to get that monkey off their back. You might be surprised at the nice, outwardly successful people who are chemically dependent slaves. Then again, if you've had much experience of the world, you probably wouldn't be.

Mainly people came to Serenity House not because of the books Joe McQuany would write, or lectures he would give, or the programs he devised, but because of Joe himself. To quote one of his coworkers and admirers-but we repeat ourselves-his soft, unjudging brown eyes would connect with the souls of others. Joe seemed to look past all the superficialities that separate us from one another and see within the whole creature, sinner man.

You may have met people like Joe on rare occasion-if you've been fortunate. They've got something special about them, a kind of almost palpable aura. And you never forget them. They're always there for you; they're always there for everybody. The short word for them may be saints.

The man never tired, not even during his last, four-year struggle with Parkinson's, and he never stopped dreaming. His last great dream was a treatment center for women. When the ground was broken for that project two years ago, and folks asked where the money was coming from to finish it, Joe told the paper: "I had $300 [when I started]. People said, 'How are you gonna do it?' I said, 'I don't know,' and I stepped out. I've always stepped out into things, and people have always helped me."

They did again. Construction was completed a few weeks ago, and Joe was there to admire the finished work. It was another of his dreams achieved.

He didn't seem surprised. Sitting on a patio overlooking the new building just days before he went into the hospital for the last time, Joe McQuany kicked back and observed, "It's gonna be okay." JOE McQUANY could have been talking about a lot more than a building; he could have been summing up the message he'd brought to so many, whatever their station in life, who were poor in spirit. Then they would read one of his books, or leave one of his lectures renewed and resolved, or check out of Serenity House rich in hope and determination. That might've been all they had, but they knew it was going to be enough, it was gonna be okay. A short word for that attitude is faith.

Joe taught folks faith, or rather he would let them come to it. Much as someone might point out the quality of the light on a beautiful fall day, or a harvest moon shining above, or the grace all around us. When it came to knowing how to live a full life free and unhindered, Joe McQuany was his own best example.

At his death last week, condolences poured in from all over, including nearly every state in the Union and 10 foreign countries at last count. His obituary noted that Joseph Daniel McQuany left behind his wife of 48 years, Loubelle, numerous family (including 12 greatgrandchildren), and "friends around the world." Many of those friends have the best of reasons to be grateful for Joe: a life of their own-rather than one dictated by the current addiction.

Joe always lived simply. He was interested in a richer life: helping others. Reading this today may be someone out there who is heavy-burdened, convinced that if it weren't for the particular chemical cross he has to bear, he'd live fully, do great things, amount to something. In 1962 Joe McQuany found himself in that spot, desperate over his weakness, and proceeded to . . . turn it into a strength. So can you, Troubled Reader. "If I hadn't been an alcoholic, I probably would have amounted to nothing."

Editorial used with permission, ©2007, Arkansas Democrat-Gazette

11/02/2007

References

Alcoholics Anonymous, 3rd edition, New York: Alcoholics Anonymous World Services, Inc., 1976. (The "Big Book")

Alcoholics Anonymous Comes of Age: A Brief History of A.A., New York: Alcoholics Anonymous Publishing, Inc., 1957.

Twelve Steps and Twelve Traditions, New York: Alcoholics Anonymous World Services, Inc, 1981. (The "Twelve and Twelve")

Recovery Dynamics, 2nd edition, Little Rock, Arkansas, Kelly Foundation, 1989

Addresses

Alcoholics Anonymous World Services, Inc.
P.O. Box 459
Grand Central Station
New York, New York 10163
www.aa.org

Al-Anon WSO
1600 Corporate Landing
Virginia Beach, VA 23454
www.al-anon.org

Kelly Foundation
2801 West Roosevelt Road
Little Rock, AR 72204
www.kellyfdn.com